To Ruth Haney
"Happy Birthday" (1997)

Aren't we thankful to God,
for each time of "refreshing"
or another very CLOSE ENCOUNTER
with our wonderful Lord? Amen!
　　　Love,
　　Virginia Conley

Close Encounters Knowing the Savior

Close Encounters Knowing the Savior

Paul Smith

VISION™ HOUSE
PUBLISHING, INC.
Gresham, Oregon 97030

CLOSE ENCOUNTERS
© 1995 by Paul Smith

Published by Vision House Publishing Inc.
1217 NE Burnside Rd.
Suite 403
Gresham, Oregon 97030

Printed in the United States of America

Unless otherwise indicated, Scripture references are from the Holy Bible: New
International Version, copyright 1973, 1978, 1984 by the International Bible
Society. Used by permission of Zondervan Bible Publishers.

ISBN: 1-885305-27-3

95 96 97 98 99 00 01—08 07 06 05 04 03 02 01

FOREWORD

From a lifetime of involvement with college students, I have learned that they do not necessarily dismiss as irrelevant the proclamation of the Word of God. But they long for some tangible evidence that this Word can be lived as well as preached. In this they are not alone. Our society is understandably disillusioned by promises that are not kept, statements that are proved false, and examples that are notorious for a studied repudiation of traditional values.

Thankfully, the Biblical record includes accounts of individuals strikingly similar to us today whose lives were dramatically altered because of the transforming power of the Living Christ. Unfortunately, for most of our contemporaries, the Bible is a closed book with its message shrouded in cognitive darkness. In recognition of this age-old problem, God ordained that His Word should be declared by those whom He called to this task and, then, by His Holy Spirit endowed with insight, understanding, and dynamic authority in application. Paul Smith is one of this number.

His writing reflects rigorous scholarship blended with creative imagination in the exposition of the Biblical text. It also discloses his own thoughtful interaction with the Author of that text. Some would call it "seeking the Lord," contemplation that produces the inspiration characteristic of what the Apostle John identifies as the "anointing."

This distinguishes ministry from being merely descriptive. Instead, it is a testimonial of personal engagement with God and his Word. It is also a demonstration of confidence that the same Holy Spirit who has transformed a fallible human being into one who speaks for God also attunes the perceptions of those who are to hear that Word from Him. This confidence in substantial measure is derived from the Scriptural narrative recounting what happened to those whose lives were vitally affected by their contact with the Savior. It is also rooted in the author's own experience of growing in the grace and knowledge of our Lord Jesus Christ.

That is why I commend this book to you. It documents Paul Smith's commitment to the trustworthiness and transforming power of God's Word as evidenced by the miracle of grace in his life and in the lives of key individuals in the Biblical accounts.

May this book and its author furnish to a watching world the corroboration of the Scriptural claims that our culture needs to see. And may you find in reading this volume a word from the Lord that will enable you to be a "living epistle" to be read and known by all who see you. Cecil Alexander has expressed well what our summons is:

Jesus calls us o'er the tumult of our life's wild, restless sea, Day by day His sweet voice soundeth, saying, "Christian, follow Me."

Hudson T. Armerding

Quarryville, Pennsylvania

October 3, 1995

CONTENTS

In the first century A.D., a man appeared walking along the dusty byways of a land that had sat for centuries at the crossroad of civilizations.

As improbable as it may seem, this man, the itinerant son of a village carpenter, a man who never held any office, who never authored a single document, who never traveled more than 250 miles from his place of birth, and who never commanded much of a following during his lifetime, would absolutely and irrevocably change the course of history! And he would do it primarily through the breath-taking power of an absolutely consistent and holy life, climaxed—as his followers excitedly proclaimed—by his actual resurrection from the dead! Anything less than this would not explain his tremendous impact on human history.

Wouldn't it have been marvelous to have actually met him! The Christian church today struggles to represent him adequately. But what if we had actually met him? What effect might such an encounter have had on our lives? How might it have altered our course? Would we be the person we are today?

The people who did meet Jesus firsthand were a diverse lot, not unlike ourselves. What if we begin by asking them to tell us about their experiences? Perhaps we will be able to see Jesus in a fresh way through their eyes. With Peter we may encounter him while standing knee-deep in murky water, or again with Nicodemus in a thoughtful conversation on the rooftop, enjoying the evening breeze. After Pentecost, the nature of our encounter will change as we meet him in the person of his Holy Spirit, just as we might today! Perhaps at first we will miss the point, as did Simon Magus, much to his chagrin. Or perhaps we will share the wonder and relief of the good Cornelius.

But whoever we allow to introduce us to Christ, let me underscore something terribly important from the outset. *There is no reason in the world why their experience with Jesus cannot be our own!* We are talking about real people here who lived in space and time and history, who encountered Jesus Christ and whose lives were irrevocably transformed. There is no reason why the wonderful, sweeping transformation of their lives cannot be our experience as well. We need no secret formula, no arcane ritual; we do not even need to be particularly astute theologically, certainly not at the outset. We must simply come in the same spirit in which they came to encounter the person, the unique and compelling person of this man Jesus!

Let me sound a warning, however. There is a risk in this adventure, You will not be able to read these eyewitness accounts simply as a matter of curiosity. For Jesus will meet *you* here. If he is a person worth considering at all, he is a person living today, and not restricted by any means from placing the same challenge before you which he placed before them. This is not ultimately about someone else's encounter with Jesus. It is about yours and mine. And to encounter Jesus is to see your own life in cosmic perspective. It must make a difference!

The real tragedy, however, would be if, like King Agrippa, who was terrified by his close encounter through the persuasive witness of the apostle Paul, we were to back away from this one great opportunity to set our lives on course for eternity because the immediate personal cost seemed too great. What a tremendous waste that would be!

But if you are bold enough, I invite you to come with me for a close and personal encounter with the Savior.

CHAPTER ONE

What If He Knew Me?

Peter
(Luke 5:1–11)

I t was a grand day, really, with the sun reflecting off the sparkling blue waters of Lake Gennesaret, the gem of Galilee; its sapphire surface nestled in a setting of rich green hills. The name Gennesaret actually means "garden of abundance." Josephus, historian and contemporary of Jesus, describes the area as "an immense garden of incomparable fertility" rife with luscious date palms, and trees bent heavy with oranges, figs, pomegranates, olives, almonds and all kinds of nuts. Fragrant balsam and cypress flourished along with castor bean trees.

If you were to visit today, you would find the northwestern shore of the Sea of Galilee to be quiet and pastoral. A low, empty plain reaches back from the shore about two miles toward the mountains that recede into the distance.

But in Jesus' day this narrow coastal plain was one of the most densely populated areas in all of Palestine. Thousands of people lived in a string of perhaps a dozen thriving cities along the coast, where they harvested the abundant fruits and the profusion of fish with which the warm, clear waters of the Sea of Galilee teemed.

On this particular morning one of those fishermen, a big, burly, energetic man called Simon, was working diligently along the shore where he and his partners had stretched their nets over several of the black basalt boulders at water's edge. Simon was quite unaware of the quaint beauty of the nearby village of Capernaum, or of the low, wooded hills behind them, or of the impressive, snow-covered summit of Mount Hermon to the north. He was tired from fishing all night, and he had work to do, cleaning the nets.

Besides, this was all familiar to him. He had been born in Bethsaida, just a few miles to the east, beyond the Jordan's inlet to the lake. But when that sleepy little fishing village was rebuilt by Herod's son and dedicated to the Roman Caesar, it had taken on a distinctively pagan culture. So Simon and his brother Andrew had been glad for the opportunity to leave.

In Capernaum, they had become partners in a fishing business owned by a man named Zebedee. Along with Zebedee's two sons, James and John, they committed themselves to the trade of supplying fish for the population. Zebedee, being a rather wealthy and industrious man, marketed his product extensively in Jerusalem, where he had many business contacts.

Tired and preoccupied as he was, however, Simon was distracted by the drama unfolding around him that morning. A great crowd of people had gathered and seemed to be growing with each passing minute. Periodically, I can imagine, Simon cursed and waved back some overzealous spectator scrambling over the rocks and threatening to tangle his nets.

The object of all this attention was Jesus, a man Simon had met a year earlier when his brother Andrew had brought him excitedly to the shores of the Jordan river to introduce them. Andrew was convinced Jesus was the Messiah. Simon was uncertain, but he had been impressed with this lean and sun-burned man. There was something about him that appealed to Simon, and they had certainly made a connection. In fact, Jesus had given him a nickname, Peter (or Cephas in the Aramaic), meaning "rock." Simon Peter was uncertain why the name was chosen, but was flattered by the personal attention. The name had stuck.

In fact, Simon and Andrew—having some time off from fishing in that Jewish sabbatical year of 28 A.D.—had traveled a bit with Jesus. People had begun to proclaim him a prophet, and Peter had to admit he had seen him do some pretty remarkable things. At a wedding in Cana, Jesus turned several great pitchers of water into wine, and since then Peter had seen him heal a number of people, including Peter's own mother-in-law. The remarkable thing was that he did it with such natural and irresistible authority. He simply spoke, or touched, and people were healed or demons were cast out. It was an astonishing thing!

Sabbatical over, Simon and Andrew had returned to Zebedee and the fishing business, but regularly they heard reports of Jesus' growing reputation. Over in Nazareth, Jesus' own hometown, he had been thrown out of the synagogue for teachings that seemed to border on blasphemy. But nearly everywhere the common people spoke of him with awe and respect.

Now he had recently come here to Capernaum, where he took the population by storm. Everyone was talking about his wonderful miracles and astonishing authority. This particular morning he had come down to the waterfront, and now the crowd was practically pushing him into the lake as they jostled one another in an attempt to see and hear him. Working in the crowded space along the shore, Simon Peter listened to Jesus talk about the kingdom of God as if it were a place with which he was intimately familiar. It would be great, Peter thought, to have time to contemplate such things, but a man had to earn a living. Besides, Peter admitted, if *he* had anything to do with who got into such a kingdom, he certainly wouldn't let a calloused old sinner like himself inside! He tried to live right, of course, and having family responsibilities had mellowed him a bit, but the people he worked with were a tough lot, and someone was always there to take advantage of you. Peter was not one to back down. If Jesus had really known what Peter's heart was like—Peter thought—he wouldn't have invited him along on his travels a year earlier. He bent to his work with the nets.

"Simon." Peter looked up, surprised to hear his name on the lips of this famous man. Jesus had climbed into Simon and Andrew's boat. The crowd had made it impossible for him to stand on the shore any longer. "Would you push out a bit from the shore?" Jesus asked. Peter scrambled down into the water to the side of the boat. Uncoiling several loops of rope from the stone anchor, he pushed the wooden boat out several yards into the shallow water. Jesus sat down and continued teaching the people from the boat.

When he had finished speaking, he called to Simon once again, "Put out into deep water, and let down the nets for a catch." Peter was surprised. This was not the best time of the day for fishing, and besides, they had already been out all night and had just now gotten everything cleaned up. "Master, we've worked hard all night and haven't caught anything—" Peter could not resist saying, "but because you say so, I will let down the nets."

Peter signaled his brother Andrew and a couple of the hired helpers, and they loaded the nets back into the boat, pulled up the anchor, and began to row back out through the crowded harbor toward the deep water. Once clear of the other boats, the helpers yanked at the knots, unfurling the sail, which dropped from the yardarms. The sail filled with the warm, offshore breeze, driving the boat forward as the prow cut easily through the water. A short distance from shore, Jesus instructed them to furl the sail once more and let down the nets. They did, no doubt somewhat skeptically, for they must have wondered how a carpenter could know more about fishing than they did. But immediately their purse seine enclosed a great shoal of fish, so large, we are told, that the net began to break.

Signaling frantically to James and John on the shore, Peter and his shipmates struggled until the two boats, now loaded so heavily that they were beginning to ship water, finally made it back to land.

There everyone made a grand commotion, transferring the fish to containers in which they would be hauled to the market and exclaiming about the astonishing catch. Peter, however, usually at the center of every activity, stood apart from the turmoil. What was happening with the fish did not interest him any longer. Peter's eyes were fixed on Jesus, who stood quietly to one side, searching the faces of the excited fishermen.

Suddenly Peter realized that those eyes that could see a shoal of fish concealed in the dark depths of the lake could see the hoard of sins concealed in the dark depths of his soul as well. He found himself reviewing all the coarse, insensitive words he had ever spoken. He remembered the shameful conversations he often had with the rough crowd who bought his fish. He thought about how many times he had stretched the truth to extend his profit margin. Wincing with the pain of it all, he reflected on how thoughtless and selfish he had often been with his wife, and how many ugly and degrading thoughts he had allowed to harbor in his mind. He began to remember dark, troubling sins long forgotten, and now—with an overwhelming sense of his own guilt and failure—knew that he did not want those eyes turned upon him. (You and I, all of us, can hold our heads up in public only because no one really knows what goes on in the depths of our hearts.)

With a sense of shame approaching panic, Peter fell at

Jesus' knees crying, "Depart from me, O Lord, for I am a sinful man."

But Jesus looked into Peter's eyes, and it was apparent that his gaze did indeed plumb the depths of Peter's soul, but there was great compassion in those eyes, and not even a trace of condemnation. He could see Peter's grief over his sins, and knew the fear and the pain welling up in Peter's troubled soul meant that he was just the sort of person who would appreciate his gift of grace. Jesus said, gently, "Don't be afraid [Peter]; from now on you will catch men." There was such a look of confidence and grace in Jesus' eyes that Peter was vanquished. If this man could look into his polluted soul and still love him, Peter in that moment knew that he could not be any place other than at this man's side. All his life he had managed to live with himself mostly by avoiding facing who he really was. But here was a man who *did* know who he really was. Here was a man who saw every slimy little sin crawling around in the dark ocean of his soul, and who could deal with that and not only love him the way we might love some poor, pitiful creature who can't help himself, but love him in a way that showed he believed Peter was a valuable person, a person who could do something grandly worthwhile.

It was more than Peter could ever have dreamed. He knew he would follow this man anywhere. There was no price too great to pay, no price that seemed like a price at all, in taking Jesus' hand to walk with him.

———— ⟋⟍⟋⟍ ————

Perhaps you, like Peter, consider yourself an average person, a hard worker, not particularly intellectual, not very religious or inclined to engage in much philosophical speculation, maybe a person with a family to support and a demanding job that consumes most of your time and energy.

More to the point, perhaps you feel that while you are

basically an honest person, there are many hidden sins that mar your own soul and separate you from God. You feel that if people could know who you really are, they would recognize your hypocrisy and reject you. The road you have walked in your life has gradually eroded your innocence and you feel you have lost the opportunity for a life of purity and power.

Let Peter's experience be a source of inspiration for you. Peter's life wasn't transformed overnight. In fact, some time later when he had the opportunity to prove his courage and commitment by standing with Jesus at his trial, he failed miserably. But on this particular day, Peter took the first essential step toward the transformation that would make his one of the most compelling witnesses in all history. Just as importantly, he made the commitment that would guarantee him an exhilarating renewal, penetrating to the very depths of his sin-contaminated soul. That day, for the first time in his life, Peter could breathe the fresh air of God's grace and feel the relief of sins forgiven, of the burden lifted from his shoulders. He could feel the liberating power of God's Spirit unleashed in his life.

You can know the very same relief and the very same power! What it will require of you is precisely what it required of Peter. It will require, first, the acknowledgment of your sinfulness. This would seem a simple enough confession, but in our day of fierce self-advancement and self-promotion, many people have great difficulty admitting their sinfulness. Nevertheless, you should know that there can never be renewal in your life without this fundamental acknowledgment. You will spend your whole life dragging your burden of sin with you unless you deal with it.

Second, we must recognize, as Peter did, that the possibility for lasting change in our lives comes only through the person of Jesus Christ. Because it was in him alone that God appeared and walked among us, it is through him alone that we can be reconciled to the God from whom we have become estranged by our sin and rebellion. No one else in history has brought God's grace and power to us directly and personally—the grace and power that can utterly transform a life and ultimately raise us even from the dead!

Finally, we must see, as Peter did, that regardless of who we are, regardless of where we have been, regardless of anything in our past history, the only pathway that will lead us to this forgiveness and transformation is the one we walk in the company of Jesus Christ. Like Peter, we must be willing to commit ourselves to walk with Jesus wherever he leads us, or we will never find our way into the kingdom of God.

I believe with all my heart that there is not a person who hears this story who does not have the potential for the sort of transformation that made Peter into such a compelling and effective man.

But if you and I are to know that transforming power, we too must walk the pathway that Peter walked. We must confess our sinfulness honestly before the Lord, we must acknowledge the salvation that lies only in Christ Jesus, and we, too, must commit our lives to walk with him wherever he leads us.

Ready for a Change

~•~

Matthew
(Luke 5:27–32)

Levi, known to us by his Greek name Matthew, would have been one of the wealthiest, if not one of the most popular, men in his hometown of Capernaum. Capernaum was a border town and the location of one of three main tax offices in Palestine. Levi worked at the customs office, collecting taxes for the Roman occupational government.

The gathering of taxes has never been particularly popular. But under the circumstances that prevailed in Israel, the task—and those who performed it—would have been even more repugnant. Certain wealthy entrepreneurs had paid a fixed sum of money to the Roman government for the privilege of levying taxes and tolls upon exports and imports, as well as any goods that passed through the territory. The entrepreneurs would hire "publicans" or tax collectors whose profit came from assessing whatever the traffic would bear. Obviously the situation was ripe for abuse.

Although Matthew himself was Jewish, he would have been considered a traitor by his countrymen because he served the pagan Roman government, and also because he made a very good living off their productivity. Most were sure they had never known an honest tax collector. Bribes and extortion were commonplace. There was nothing good to be said about such a parasite.

Simon Peter and the other disciples whom Jesus had already called to follow him would have known Matthew well—too well, I think Peter might have complained. Every time Simon arrived at shore with his catch of fish, Matthew or his assistants were there to skim the revenue for the Roman government.

But Matthew was an intelligent and observant man, well versed in the Hebrew Scriptures, and quite aware of the stir Jesus was causing in his community. He would most likely have been at the synagogue a few days earlier when Jesus had cast a demon out of one of his fellow townsmen—and he must have been impressed as the streets filled with people at sundown on the Sabbath and Jesus worked late into the night healing and blessing and touching and encouraging all who came.

Later Matthew would write that it seemed to him as if the prophecy of Isaiah concerning the "Suffering Servant," where he said "He took up our infirmities and carried our diseases" was being fulfilled. So Matthew had watched Jesus, and knowing the Scriptures as he did, he had begun to wonder if this remarkable man who had recently arrived in his city might not be specially anointed by God.

On the day Matthew's life was to change, however, he was busy with his books and the supervision of his assistants as they counted the flocks of sheep and goats and weighed the barrels of fish and produce. As people came and went, Matthew hardly looked up from his work. He had become immune over the years to the complaints and curses of his countrymen. He had a job to do, that was all. If they didn't like it, that was their problem.

But sometime during the day, through the confusion of braying donkeys, bleating sheep, and berating countrymen, Matthew became aware that someone had just called his name, and the tone of this voice was far different from the way Matthew normally was addressed. Looking up, he found himself staring into the eyes of the very man, Jesus.

Up to that moment Matthew may have been quite certain that he could remain an anonymous observer. He was a quiet man. In fact, he is the only well-known disciple who is never directly quoted by others. The New Testament opens with his written account of the life of Jesus, but I think we would have considered Matthew the one man in a crowd who was generally content to keep his mouth shut and his eyes open. There was a certain self-protection in his reticence; he could weigh what was going on around him without becoming accountable for his own position.

But now—suddenly—he could remain anonymous no longer. Jesus was looking him in the eye. In front of all these people, Jesus was asking him for a response. Matthew had thought he could observe all the activity from the safe haven of his customs post, perhaps justifying his own dishonesty and his contempt for the people as part of a necessary job, but at this moment all his excuses dissolved.

Here, before this wonderful man whom Matthew had seen giving himself so unreservedly for others, Matthew had to admit that he had spent his entire life serving himself. Indeed, he had spent his entire life deceiving himself.

"Follow me," Jesus was saying—saying to *him*—to Matthew, the person his own people wanted to avoid. *"Come,"* Jesus was saying, "and be my disciple." I believe something in Jesus' eyes must have told him he could put all his misspent life behind him at that moment and everything could be new. If there was a price, even a great price, no matter. The compensation would be greater still.

I can imagine Matthew looking around the customs house. Here was the source of his wealth and security. Here was the occupation that supported his affluent lifestyle. Here was the one business he knew anything about. But here also was the source of his unpopularity, the source of his cynicism about life, the source of his haunting sense of guilt that what he was doing with his life was not worthwhile; in fact, it was damaging to others. Matthew must have thought it would be wonderful to walk away from this ugly business and have a sense that he could make his life worthwhile. Wouldn't it be wonderful to feel that his hands were clean for once in his life and his heart was pure? Wouldn't it be wonderful to cast his lot with the most remarkable man history had ever known?

Matthew shook his head slowly, glanced once more around the booth, then—patting his chief assistant on the back—said he was leaving early . . . and wouldn't be back. The man must have looked stunned as Matthew stepped out of the toll house and walked up to Jesus. Jesus, I suspect, was looking at him as if to say, "I knew it. I knew you had it in you. I knew you were more than a tax collector at heart. You won't regret this decision."

That night the rest of the disciples made their way hesitantly to the wealthy suburb where Matthew lived. He had invited them to a great feast and had invited many of his friends and fellow tax collectors. The disciples may have been self-conscious about their appearance, and quite unsure how to conduct themselves in this stratum of society. The large, luxurious rooms of Matthew's house with their silk hangings and brocade furniture were quite unlike the simple life most common laborers enjoyed. The gathering included sophisticated and very pagan revelers. It was not the society in which the disciples normally circulated.

For Jesus, however, there was no problem. He seemed perfectly at ease accepting Matthew's lavish hospitality, and throughout the evening engaged his pagan friends in animated, challenging conversation. They listened to him talk openly and sincerely about the love of God for them and the possibility of new beginnings for those who would turn from their sin and follow him. And they had to admit they were sinners . . . yet their hearts were somehow drawn to this man. They could see the compelling attraction of his transparent witness. I think they knew why their friend Matthew had just announced that he was giving up his position and would be selling all he had to go and to support the ministry of this man Jesus.

Before the evening was quite over, some of Jesus' disciples slipped outside, probably to escape their own discomfort in the presence of these irreligious folks. Once outside, however, the disciples encountered some of the scribes and Pharisees, who immediately began to challenge them about eating and drinking with tax collectors and sinners. The disciples did not know what to say. For all we know, they were probably inclined to agree! But, as they stood there in the darkness trying to think of a defense for their master, Jesus stepped out from the house and approached with an irrefutable reply. "Those who are well have no need of a physician," he said, "but those who are sick; I have not come to call the righteous, but sinners to repentance."

It was not, of course, that Jesus had nothing to offer the religious folks or those who were self-satisfied. It was just that he knew that only those who understood their need, only those who understood the disease of their own souls would ever look to him for a cure. Until they were ready for a change, there was little he could do to help them.

Matthew had been ready for a change. The road he had been walking down most of his life had at first seemed to lead toward his goals of happiness and prosperity. But as time went along, he began to wonder. Prosperity, yes, this road had led to a considerable degree of prosperity. He owned a fine home filled with wonderful things, and he moved in an elite group in the community. But prosperity had not brought him happiness—and what was anything worth if it could not bring some happiness and contentment into your soul?

Actually it had taken him some time to recognize the many reasons to seek happiness elsewhere. He *had* thought he was happy at first. But the more time that went by, the more he realized that happiness lay in being loved by someone. Matthew was loved by no one. Happiness lay in having a sense that he deserved someone's respect, and Matthew didn't believe he deserved anyone's respect. Most especially, happiness lay in giving happiness to someone else, and Matthew had never given happiness to anyone. Ironically, the more he tried to grasp at happiness for himself, the more it eluded him. But what he saw in Jesus' example was that the deepest peace and contentment were directly related to the giving of love.

So the time had come for Matthew to change the course of his life, and he knew it. The word Jesus chooses to describe this change is *metanoia*. It is translated "repentance" in the NIV and in most versions, but it is a much stronger word than that. Repentance only describes the negative side of this action—our sorrow for our sins, and our willingness to turn from our evil ways. But there is an important, positive side to *metanoia* as well. One must not only turn away from sin, but very positively and resolutely turn *to* God in obedience and faith and trust. The word describes a complete transformation, a change of mind, heart, will, and conduct—turning from one road to another.

A few months before my wife and I were married, I was moving across country with all my earthly belongings in my car. On a particularly rainy and desolate night, I found myself trying to get through New York City. With visibility near zero I detoured around construction zones, tried to read street signs caked with grime, and felt as if I were being sucked into a giant black hole somewhere on the Jersey side of the Hudson River. I had started out on the right track, I thought, and I continued merrily on my way rather enjoying the adventure. But when I finally figured out that this course would not get me to my destination in quaint and beautiful New England, I understood that there were two vitally important things to be done. The sooner I did them, the better off I would be.

First, I had to get *off* this course, which seemed likely to deposit me in the Hackensack River. Second, I had to get *on* the course that would eventually take me to my desired destination. Both actions were equally important.

It seems to me this was Matthew's experience also at the moment he encountered Jesus. He saw the right road—the engaging path of selfless generosity represented by Jesus Christ—at the very time he was coming to realize that his own path offered him nothing of ultimate value. If he was ready for a change, then Jesus could help him. Matthew was ready to abandon the path guaranteed to make him richer and more miserable and commit himself without reservation to this man who alone could make his life worth living.

In the days that followed, many of Matthew's friends found it difficult to believe the price he paid to follow Christ— giving up status and a lucrative tax business seemed an enormous price to them. They may not have understood that Matthew felt it had cost him nothing—nothing more than the abandonment of a path that was sucking him into his own black hole. And that was a price he was more than happy to pay. We don't hear Matthew complain at all.

———————

I don't know what path you are on in your life right now, but perhaps this would be a good time to step back and consider your destination. You only get to live your life one time, and it is critically important that you ask yourself periodically "What am I doing with my life?" We get rushed along by the current of our activities and expectations, and we often fail to consider what is at the other end of the path.

Where is your life headed? Now is the time to examine your direction, not after your course has been established. Are you on a path that is truly satisfying to you? A path that leads to something good? Will people say of you, "Now there is a person whose life made a difference." And how will the God who created you evaluate your life? We avoid such questions, but they are the most significant questions we can ask about our lives.

Until we recognize that our lives have fallen short of our own expectations—let alone God's—we will not be ready for change. But when we *are* ready, let me assure you there are magnificent possibilities in walking with Jesus Christ. Just think about Matthew—the aloof, self-serving public official who was rich in the world's goods, but poverty-stricken in his own soul. He might well have lived and died in obscurity, able to afford a lavish funeral, but with no one to mourn his passing. Yet when he decided he was ready to risk everything for a change, and came to follow Jesus Christ, Matthew left his name not only in history, but in eternity. He wrote one of the most beautiful and thoughtful accounts of the life of Jesus, one that has been instrumental in changing millions of lives for the better. He even gave his very name "Matthew" a wonderful reputation that has survived him by nearly 2,000 years. We love his name because this man, this petty public official, this taciturn, self-serving man encountered Jesus Christ and said, "It's time to change."

The transformation in the lives of the people we meet on the pages of the New Testament can easily be the transformation in your life. These were normal people. They were not different from us. They were not great saints with halos hovering over their heads. They were normal people with normal intelligence and normal skills, living life very much as you and I are living it. But they made a decision to leave the pathway of self-indulgence and sin, and give their lives wholeheartedly to Jesus Christ. And that is what made the difference.

This giving of self does not mean all of us will have to change careers, though of course there may be some occupations in which we ought not to be involved. But Jesus needs salt and light everywhere in the world. The question isn't leaving one vocation for another. The question is leaving the occupation of serving ourselves for the occupation of serving Jesus Christ—a challenge to which all of us can respond.

We, too, stand before Jesus. Whatever we have been doing—busy with our own activities, hardly hearing the voices and the confusion around us—in the middle of all this Jesus looks us in the eye and says, "Matthew . . . Mary . . . John . . . follow me."

And we have the same opportunity to respond.

What path are you walking today? What path will make a difference in your life? What path will lead to the ultimate peace and fulfillment and joy that you desire with all your heart? What path would God have you walk? Just as He called Matthew, Jesus is calling you to follow Him.

How will you answer?

The Mind and the Spirit

Nicodemus
(John 3:1–16)

Across the rooftops of the city to the west lay a faint, reddish incandescence, low on the horizon, as if the Judean hills that had baked in the white-hot sun all day were now radiating that heat back into the heavens. Against the deep blue canopy of the sky the evening stars had begun to appear. Directly overhead was Arcturus, the "Bear Watcher" in the constellation Bootes, keeping a wary eye on the Great Bear to the north.

It had been a hot and exhausting day, but now Jesus was relaxing on the rooftop of his friends' home in Jerusalem, enjoying the cooling breeze that had begun to stir just about sundown. He rested on a wooden bench behind a parapet of the lovely limestone house, waiting for a guest who had requested the opportunity to meet with him in private. Before long, Jesus saw the man appear at the top of the stairs, escorted by a servant. The newcomer thanked his escort and came on resolutely across the rooftop toward this man—the one who was creating such a stir in Jerusalem.

As Jesus watched this fellow come, he thought how different he was from the young men who had already begun to accompany him in his ministry. Somewhat older, this man Nicodemus was a wealthy, established member of the Jewish ruling council, the Sanhedrin. Unlike Peter and his companions, who were what we would call "blue-collar workers"— tough tradesmen who worked with their hands—Nicodemus was a scholar and an intellectual. And unlike Matthew, who had made no secret of his pagan lifestyle, Nicodemus was a very religious man, a member of the sect of the Pharisees who studied the law and took it very seriously. In fact, they took a vow that they would uphold the law in its every detail. As a member of the ruling council, the supreme court of the Jews, Nicodemus would have earned considerable respect and firmly established status in the community.

The fact that Nicodemus, a respected teacher of the law, would deign to come to Jesus, this renegade, unschooled teacher, was an indication that Nicodemus was open-minded— a truly liberal thinker in the best sense of the word. He was willing to look for truth no matter what its source. He had been impressed both with the depth of Jesus' teaching and with the remarkable accompanying miracles. In his constant search for the truth, Nicodemus wanted to learn more.

After the customary greetings Nicodemus sat across from Jesus. Nicodemus began by addressing Jesus as "Rabbi"—a cordial term for a teacher; a compliment to Jesus.

Rabbi, we know you are a teacher who has come from God. For no one could perform the miraculous signs you are doing if God were not with him.

Jesus sensed that Nicodemus was a man on an honest search. Did he arrange this night meeting because fraternizing with Jesus would have been frowned on in his circle, or did he arrange it because he really wanted uninterrupted time with Jesus—time that would allow him to ask questions and reflect upon the answers?

Nicodemus needed time with Jesus away from the swirling crowds. He needed time to think, he needed time to ask good questions, time to consider Jesus' response, time to engage Jesus in debate, time to address his own doubts, time ultimately to pursue the truth. And, as we see, Jesus respected Nicodemus' unique quest for truth.

Contrast this with what we have seen with the previous two men. To establish credibility with Peter, what did Jesus do? He went fishing with him! Matthew had needed to be confronted with the necessity for change, so Jesus did that. But with Nicodemus, Jesus would happily engage in sophisticated, quiet, intellectual discussion befitting the nature of the seeker.

This account, then, is not of a dramatic transformation in a person's life, but of a quiet, thoughtful discussion between a seeker and a master.

Still, Nicodemus was not without intellectual pride. Jesus knew that he would need to lead the scholar beyond the limits of his own thinking, beyond the confines of his own narrowly defined orthodoxy, which included the belief that salvation could be attained by meticulously observing the finest points of the law.

Commitment to a scrupulously lawful life was admirable. But Jesus leapt to the heart of the debate with this challenge: "I tell you the truth, no one can see the kingdom of God unless he is born again." My guess is that Nicodemus' initial reaction to that was about as enthusiastic as is the response of most intellectuals today when told of the need to be "born again." They say, "I want to think this through. I want to use my mind. I want to come to an intelligent conclusion. Don't talk to me about being born again." But that is precisely what Jesus told Nicodemus he needed to think about.

He knew that Nicodemus sincerely desired to be a part of God's kingdom, and that through an enormous effort of the will this man had attempted to place himself under the rule of God by his commitment to law-keeping. That was admirable, and I am sure Jesus respected him for it. But Jesus knew as well that this careful conduct would never resolve the deeper issues of the human heart. One could keep all the laws on the surface and still have a prideful or resentful spirit, a spirit of bitterness. Sinful attitudes could be just as destructive as sinful conduct. No, the heart would have to change before there could be a genuine and permanent change in a person's conduct.

With a single sentence, Jesus presented the main challenge to any person who depends on his or her own wisdom to do what is right. Not only will all our efforts fail to satisfy the requirements of a holy God, but the person who seeks God in that way hasn't a clue what the kingdom of God is really all about.

The kingdom of God may include only those who have undergone a change so radical it can only be described as being born all over again, born from above, as the term suggests—remade in one's spirit. For all of our efforts, for all of our careful reflection and thought, unless our spirits are remade, we will not understand and we will not enter the kingdom of God.

Nicodemus, for all his brilliance, did not understand. How can a man be born when he is old? Surely he cannot enter a second time into his mother's womb to be born! Nicodemus was intelligent enough to know that Jesus was not speaking literally here, but he confesses that he does not really know what Jesus is talking about. Of course he doesn't! His eyes have not yet been opened to the things of the kingdom.

There may be a touch of wistfulness here as well. Nicodemus is struck by the analogy of being born again and reflects on how nice it would be to really get such a fresh start.

Likely you and I have also thought that way. If I had my life to live over again, how would I do it differently? We are so aware of our sins, of our mistakes, of our lack of judgment, our foolish decisions. If those things could just be erased and we could be allowed to make a fresh start, what a wonderful thing that would be!

But that kind of thinking ignores the primary issue, which is that no matter how many times we start over, we would still "foul up," we would still distort our lives, we would still make those mistakes, we would still destroy the good things God has given us. Our hearts have been distorted by sin, and so our very best efforts will always fall short. What we need is a radical transformation of our spirits so fundamental and so all-encompassing that it launches us on a new plane of living altogether.

"I tell you the truth," Jesus explains, "no one can enter the kingdom of God unless he is born of water and the Spirit. Flesh gives birth to flesh, but the Spirit gives birth to spirit." Nicodemus must understand that the problem lies precisely in our nature. Any number of natural births or fresh starts will only reintroduce us to the same problems. What we need is a genuine rebirth of the spirit—God's Spirit working to remake us from the inside. No human effort, no matter how diligent or well intentioned, will be enough. God's Spirit must raise up new life from the inside. That is where change begins. Nothing of significance will happen in our lives until that transformation takes place on the inside.

Jesus continues, "You should not be surprised at my saying, 'You must be born again.' " Seizing as he so often did on an analogy close at hand, Jesus calls Nicodemus' attention to the wind that has been picking up as they talked on the rooftop. He says, "The wind blows wherever it pleases. You hear its sound, but you cannot tell where it comes from or where it is going. So it is with everyone born of the Spirit."

Jesus has used an analogy peculiar to both the Greek and the Hebrew language, in which the word for "wind" and for "spirit" is the same. The wind, he says, is a phenomenon we may not fully comprehend, but we can certainly see its results. Precisely when and where it begins and ends may be beyond our knowledge, but that is beside the point. We have no doubt of its existence and power because of the effects we see or feel. Likewise, Jesus continues, the Spirit may not easily be explained or measured in our lives, but we ought nonetheless to see its results, recognize its power, and appreciate the accompanying potential for renewal.

Nicodemus still struggles. He engages Jesus in intellectual debate; he has known and thought about life and about how the mind and the body work for a long time. He has not yet figured out how the spirit works. I think he was quite capable of grasping the parallel between the wind and the spirit, but as an intellectual he has no concept of the nature of spiritual matters.

Here I think we run into the fundamental problem of the intellect in grasping the heart of the Christian Gospel. It *has* often been difficult for the intellectual to grasp the heart of the Christian Gospel. The intellect, vital and essential as it is, reflecting the very nature of God as it does, nonetheless is still limited. It has a category and an explanation for every phenomenon accessible to the senses. What it cannot do, however, is penetrate beyond the material world touched by our five physical senses. Thus, the attributes of the spirit are not directly accessible to the rational mind.

This is why we must not be persuaded by the scientist's pronouncement that there is no God. A scientist has no way of knowing whether there is a God or not, since the tools science uses only analyze material, quantifiable matters. As the Gospel of John explains, "God is spirit," and therefore we must approach Him in spirit. The scientist proclaiming that his observations prove there is no God is like a deaf man looking through binoculars and concluding that no such thing as music exists. He is simply using the wrong instruments. There is no way for those instruments to perceive music, but that does not prove that music does not exist.

The honest scientist must admit that his failure to see God under an electron microscope proves nothing. He is looking for a spiritual object through an instrument that only responds to physical phenomena.

This does not mean, however, that we can never know anything about God. Jesus' words to Nicodemus address our intellectual problem. "I have spoken to you of earthly things and you do not believe; how then will you believe if I speak of heavenly things?" He says he is willing to reveal himself to our physical senses if we are willing to recognize the spiritual behind the physical.

Then comes a key sentence in this conversation: "No one has ever gone into heaven except the one who came from heaven—the Son of Man." And he goes on to identify himself as the Son of Man.

He is saying that though God cannot be observed directly through the material world, though God may not be able to be grasped directly by the rational mind, nevertheless God has not left us without a knowledge of himself. For even if we cannot peer into heaven and see God, yet He may certainly reveal himself to us. The agnostic who says there is no way we could know God—that God, if He exists, is spirit, and we have no way of perceiving spiritual things—is at least being honest. What the agnostic has missed, however, is that God may well choose to reveal himself to us, and if He does we may have a clear and certain knowledge of who He is and of anything He reveals to us. (This, of course, is one of the central claims of Christianity, that God has revealed himself to us, first through the Bible and then through the Word made flesh—the person of Jesus Christ.)

It is important to see that Jesus is not asking Nicodemus to abandon his mind. Quite the contrary, Jesus honors Nicodemus' intellect with his assumption that Nicodemus could learn to think rightly about the truth. Revelation is not in conflict with intellectual truth; it simply informs the mind.

But this discussion is not simply about the mind; it is not simply a matter of understanding; it is not even simply a matter of seeing what has been revealed to us; at issue is our response to the person of Jesus. And this is where Jesus takes Nicodemus in the end.

Interestingly, he chooses a rather obscure incident from the Old Testament that illustrates the concept of trust in God's care and the provision of the Holy Spirit (the incident involving the bronze serpent) and the ability of the Spirit to accomplish His will and purpose in a yielded life.

Then finally in John 3:16 he gives an illustration, something we can see. Though we cannot see God, at least we may see his effects in our world. Though God is a Spirit and therefore not directly perceivable by our senses, nevertheless we can see what he has accomplished. And John 3:16 probably states what God has accomplished on our behalf better than any other passage of scripture—a clear revelation of what the life of Jesus was all about.

Scholars are not sure whether Jesus himself spoke these beloved words or whether this is John's interpretation as he wrote about it, but either way our attention is called to the very special act of God that demonstrates His character. Here is something tangible, understandable. He says that God loved the world so much that He gave His only begotten (His one and only) Son, that whoever believes in Him might not perish but have everlasting life (John 3:16).

He speaks here of God's initiative in loving an unlovely world. He speaks of a clear and powerful and unequivocal act of love in the sacrifice of Jesus' life to pay the penalty for our sins. And he suggests that anyone who responds with genuine belief and trust may come to know the joy and security of eternal life. Indeed, it is at this very point of coming to trust with the *heart* the truths God has revealed to the *mind* that the Holy Spirit comes to life within a person and begins to remake that person from the inside.

But notice how Jesus engaged Nicodemus where he was. Nicodemus is primarily a thinker. He was not like Peter or Matthew. Jesus affirms his intellect even as he challenges his thinking. Nicodemus then brings into his thinking new observations he may process in coming to conclusions about God and about himself.

Perhaps you have noticed that there is no word of a dramatic conversion experience for Nicodemus. If we look for something sudden and remarkable—a life abruptly transformed and moving in a new direction, we won't find it. Nicodemus apparently went away to reflect on what Jesus had said. But a wonderful process of renewal works within him as he allows his mind to be exposed to the truth.

In the seventh chapter of John's gospel we find the ruling council, of which Nicodemus is a part, meeting to debate how to stop Jesus. Some of the Pharisees have just stated rather scornfully that no one in a position of authority accepts Jesus as the Messiah. Nicodemus quite unexpectedly objects, asking if the Sanhedrin is really willing to judge a person before examining him. He risks his reputation to come to Jesus' defense. And—as we might expect—he is scorned by his colleagues for his attempt.

Having seen that something is happening in Nicodemus' life, we are not surprised to find Nicodemus in the account of Jesus' crucifixion in John 19.

Following the crucifixion he set aside all his hesitation about being identified with Jesus, and at that moment, even if it cost his reputation, even if it cost his job, even if it cost his life—which it well could—he steps forward on Jesus' behalf.

Perhaps you remember the story. Nicodemus and Joseph of Arimathea, another disciple who had kept his allegiance to Jesus a secret, decided the time had come to declare where they stood. At the very moment when the rest of the disciples had forsaken Jesus and fled, Joseph and Nicodemus risked their reputations by going to Pilate to ask for Jesus' body. They were very open and bold in taking the responsibility to prepare it for burial and lay it in a tomb. They knew their own credibility was at stake, but they had chosen to be identified with Jesus.

We do not know many details, but his actions show clearly that Nicodemus' life was transformed. He had come to trust Jesus Christ. For him it was not a dramatic moment but a gradual process that gained and grew and ultimately produced fruit in his life. The transformation in his character from a rather timid man to a man of genuine courage is particularly impressive, and we become aware that Nicodemus had a genuine, transforming encounter with Jesus Christ.

Now where do you find yourself in this story? Once again we need to ask ourselves this question. Perhaps you are quite unlike Nicodemus. Perhaps, like Peter, you have few intellectual questions that need to be answered. It is enough that you encounter the living Christ; your life will be different from that moment forward.

But perhaps, like Nicodemus, you do have serious questions about the person of Jesus and the character of faith, and the nature of truth. It is quite legitimate for you to continue to seek answers to those questions, and I do not doubt that God will honor your search, as He honored Nicodemus' search. As God is the source of all truth, I am confident that in the end His answers will satisfy. For this reason I believe Christians should never be afraid of questions directed at our faith.

Nevertheless, in the end we must understand this is much more than an intellectual search. Our very thinking needs to be transformed, along with our inner spirit. That can take place only when we are finally willing to yield our lives to Christ and to be embraced by His Spirit.

It is only when we have reached the point of yielding even our thinking to God that we will finally be able to see what His kingdom is about. Then, when His Spirit is at work within us, we will be able to enter His kingdom as well.

Amazing Faith

The Centurion
(Luke 7:1–10)

Marcellus[1] paced anxiously along the colonnaded border of the open courtyard that lay at the heart of his large home in Capernaum. He loved this place. It was beautiful here along the shores of the Sea of Galilee, where the green hills swept up to the mountains to the north and west. But more than that he loved the rural pace of life. As a young man he had lived in Rome, but he had soon grown tired of the frenetic pace of the capital city. When the opportunity came to serve as a centurion in the personal army of Herod Antipas in Galilee, he had been thrilled to accept the change.

At first the contrast was almost overwhelming—it wasn't so much the rural/urban contrast as much as the remarkable Jewish way of life compared to pagan Rome. Initially, their customs, their dress and their religion struck him as somewhat bizarre. And their provincial education and superior attitude—even though they were not as advanced as the Romans—sometimes offended him and made his adjustment difficult.

But in time he came to appreciate the Jewish people. Compared to the average Roman, the vast majority of this population lived exemplary lives! In rural Galilee, away from the more cosmopolitan Jerusalem, he came to appreciate the simplicity, the diligence, and the unaffected honesty and sincerity of the people.

To Marcellus, raised on a pagan potpourri of cynical, quarreling gods and a state religion manipulated to support the sometimes outlandish demands of the Caesars, the Jews' highly moral brand of monotheism was an invigorating breath of fresh air, and he appreciated it.

In fact, he took a personal interest in their sacred scriptures and often spent hours with some of the elders and the leaders of the synagogue discussing the right, the good and the holy. In the end, that relationship and the admiration and respect that developed led him to offer to build a new synagogue for the villagers. In this poor rural area, the people could not have afforded such a project.

They thought of him primarily as a wealthy benefactor and friend of the Jews, but Marcellus considered the donation an offering to their God, whom he had gradually come to believe was probably the true God. Whether this rather awesome and uncompromising God would accept his contribution as an act of worship from a well-meaning pagan, he did not know, but he wanted to do it anyway. At the very least it would be an expression of his genuine love for the people.

Marcellus' reflections in the courtyard were interrupted by a cry of anguish from one of the rooms nearby. He shuddered at the pain it expressed and felt the knot tightening in his stomach as he hurried toward the sound. The cries had become more frequent in the past twenty-four hours—he was afraid his servant was dying. The young man, Procorus[1], was a fine servant whom the centurion valued highly. He had come to love this young man almost as a son. When Procorus had become ill, a physician was called to let blood, but the servant's condition had only worsened. Eventually some paralysis began to set in, and the pain grew progressively more intense. Marcellus had sat by his bedside for hours at a time, stroking his arms and encouraging him to relax and breath deeply, but nothing seemed to relieve the pain or improve the young man's condition in the slightest.

But then an unexpected turn of events had injected the Roman officer with new hope. An itinerant preacher from Nazareth with an astonishing reputation for healing had just returned to Capernaum. Marcellus knew little of the Jewish teachings concerning a coming Messiah, but this man had impressed him. As the local law enforcement officer, the centurion and several of his men had been called upon more than once to keep an eye on the great crowds that surrounded the man when the power of the Lord was present in Him to heal the sick, so Marcellus had seen the man at work. He had rebuked a high fever and it had simply gone away. He had said, "Be clean!" to a leper and the flaky white skin and sores vanished. He had ordered a paralyzed man to get up and walk and he did, soliciting, as you can imagine, a chorus of astonished comments from those who witnessed it.

Marcellus' friends had told him about the first day Jesus had come to town and spoken at their new synagogue, the one he had helped build. The man's knowledge of the Scriptures was extraordinary, but what had really impressed them on that day was His authority. He spoke from God's Word as if it were He speaking. And when challenged by a man possessed of a demon, He had simply ordered it to "Come out of him!" and the demon had thrown the man down and come out without injuring him. As the demon left, however, it spoke, identifying Jesus, curiously enough, as "the Holy One of God."

As a soldier, this unassailable authority had particularly impressed the centurion. But he had also heard Jesus say to the paralyzed man on that day, "your sins are forgiven." This had seriously offended the Pharisees and teachers of the law who began to accuse Jesus of blasphemy and to say, "Who can forgive sins but God alone?" In fact, it was in response to this challenge that Jesus had told the man to get up and walk. But Marcellus had understood perfectly when Jesus said to the religious leaders, "Why are you thinking these things in your hearts? Which is easier: to say 'Your sins are forgiven,' or to say 'Get up and walk'? But that you may know that the Son of Man has authority on earth to forgive sins . . ." He said to the paralyzed man "I tell you, get up, take your mat and go home." And immediately the man stood up in front of them, picked up his mat and went home praising God.

The people were amazed, but to Marcellus it all made sense. The healing was almost incidental. What was important was what it said about the identity and authority of this man who could even forgive sins on earth.

So now when he heard that Jesus had returned to town, he had sent some of the elders of the Jews to Him to ask Him if He might come and heal Procorus. He had been waiting for their return, or for some word, when his servant had begun to cry out once again in pain. It hurt him so deeply to watch this young man's agony and not be able to do anything about it. He would have taken it upon himself if he could. It would be so wonderful if this Jesus would actually come and heal him. But of course Marcellus was very much aware that he was a Gentile and that there was a good chance no orthodox Jew would feel obligated to help him, or even think it a proper thing to do.

When Procorus finally settled back into a fitful sleep, Marcellus went to the street once again to see if anyone was coming. He had already looked down that road a dozen times that morning, but this time, a short distance away through the trees, he saw a crowd of people coming. They had been successful, then! Jesus was actually coming! What he had been hoping for so intensely—even as he steeled himself against the possibility that it might never happen—was unfolding in front of him. What a joy it would be to see his servant free from his pain and restored to health!

But then, probably to his surprise, this confident and capable centurion in the Roman army suddenly felt another emotion altogether. He became, for the first time in his life, utterly overwhelmed with a sense of his own unworthiness! After all, who was *he* in comparison to this Jesus whose time and attention and energy he sought? He had seen something of His power to heal as well as His authority over the spiritual world. He had heard snatches of His remarkable wisdom and His astonishing insight into people. He had watched Him work late into the night when He was utterly exhausted, healing all who came, and he had been impressed not so much with His stamina as with His enormous heart. Clearly what kept Him going was His great compassion for the people.

There was something of true greatness that surrounded this man. Who was Marcellus to presume upon His time and attention? Who was he, a Gentile and essentially a pagan, to ask this wonderful man, first of all to violate the time-honored custom of His own people and defile himself by entering a Gentile home? From what he knew of Jesus he suspected that He would come anyway, but it did not seem fair to have asked.

Indeed, who was he, in the end, to stand before Jesus at all? The man who could forgive sins, for God's sake! The demons had called Him "the Holy One of God!" Did they know what they were talking about? He seemed to command life with the authority one would expect from the Creator Himself, from the Creator alone! Suddenly Marcellus felt very small, very unworthy, and very unrighteous. He could not stand before this man! But what about his servant, Procorus? He did *so* want to see him healed.

Suddenly it struck him! What if Jesus simply gave the command for the disease to leave his servant! He would not have to be there to do that. He had been so impressed with this man's universal authority. Quickly he grabbed a couple of his friends who were there to help with the sick man. "Run and tell Jesus: 'Lord, don't trouble yourself, for I do not deserve to have you come under my roof. That is why I did not even consider myself worthy to come to you. But say the word, and my servant will be healed. For I myself am a man under authority, with soldiers under me. I tell this one "Go," and he goes; and that one "Come," and he comes. I say to my servant, "Do this," and he does it.'"

His commands, the centurion knew, were successful not because he himself was so powerful—he was a mid-level military man—but because the authority of the whole Roman Empire stood behind him. His word in itself could accomplish nothing were it not for the authority of the empire he represented. Jesus' authority obviously encompassed life itself! If His commands were successful, it could only be because the authority of the entire universe found its expression in Him. That alone could explain how He had the authority to say "Go," to disease and it would leave; how He had the authority to say "Come out," to a demon and it had to obey; and how He had the authority to say "Do this: take up your mat and walk," to a paralyzed man, and he was compelled to obey!

What the centurion had correctly seen—and apparently no one else had seen it so clearly—was that the issue here hinged upon Jesus' authority. Jesus was not some sort of wizard or magician, or even just a mysterious miracle worker. What he recognized in Jesus was the authority to command life. He recognized Jesus for who He was. Such authority could only come from the Creator of Life. But if God were somehow present in this man, Marcellus the centurion knew that he himself could not stand before Him. He recognized who Jesus was and he recognized who he was in relationship to this man.

Everyone else, it seemed, was content to "get a piece of the action," to draw some personal benefit from Jesus. However He pulled it off was not their concern. They just wanted to get their order in. It was sort of a "prosperity gospel" if you will: "Jesus wants us healthy and wealthy. And hey, after all, if there's something in it for me . . . I'll come!"

But you see, this is not faith, even though our materialistic age tries to define it as such. Faith focuses on the object, on the person we are learning to trust. To focus on what we can get from Him, even if it is something good, misses the point entirely. And Jesus, of course, recognized the difference in the centurion's request.

In fact, He was so impressed that this man had seen what the heart of faith was all about that he stopped, turned to the crowd following Him, and said, "I tell you, I have not found such great faith even in Israel." (It is of interest to note that only twice in the gospels is Jesus ever described as being "amazed" at something. The other time was when He was amazed at the *lack* of faith on the part of the people of Nazareth, who after all had the greatest opportunity to come to know Jesus and trust Him. This is the second expression of Jesus' amazement, but it is at *finding* faith where He might least have expected it, in a man who didn't have all the religious credentials but understood what faith was all about.)

———— ~⁓⊱⊰⁓~ ————

Jesus *does* heal the man's servant, of course, as we might expect. And often we have been content to read this passage as if it referred primarily to what we call "faith healing." But I would submit to you this morning that in fact, what we have seen here is the essence of faith; it is *saving* faith.

In Matthew's account of this same incident he describes the centurion's remarkable faith by recounting Jesus' words that in the last days "many will come from the east and the west, and will take their places at the feast of Abraham, Isaac and Jacob in the kingdom of heaven. But the subjects of the kingdom will be thrown outside, into the darkness, where there will be weeping and gnashing of teeth."

A lot of the religious folks who thought they were on the inside but never understood what faith was about will come up wanting. The only ones to be welcomed into the kingdom will be those who understood, as the centurion understood, that faith is about placing your trust in one worthy of that trust.

It seems apparent that in Jesus' eyes, what this man possessed was the sort of faith that determines how a person will spend eternity. It is the essence of all faith—we may all learn from Marcellus the attributes of faith. To believe—to have faith—is not simply a thoughtless or a passive acceptance of anything Jesus wants to do. It is rather a very specific action, a response to Jesus that involves at least three things: an awareness of one's own unworthiness, a recognition of the identity of Jesus, His supreme authority and our subsequent need to submit to that authority, and a spirit of humility in the face of such omnipotence and power manifest in the man Christ. The humility will inevitably result in a growing and genuine compassion for others. This will be the visible fruit of the faith that is forming within us.

Because the centurion responded to Jesus in all three ways, he was used as a most accurate and complete example of faith—a model that many "more religious" people, as Jesus pointed out, might pursue to their own benefit.

Notes

1 Marcellus and Procorus are both fictitious names.

The church today has carelessly accepted many counterfeit varieties of faith. Often faith is depicted as an attitude of confidence and trust that will "get you things" from God. Not only is this no true faith, it is the opposite of faith! And the test is this: Is the goal of what you call "faith" to get God to serve you, or to get you to serve God?

It is not faith to think we can command God; it is faith to recognize that God has the authority to command us. The centurion realized that Jesus' authority meant he, along with everyone else, must bow to His lordship. That is why he called Him "Lord," the strong Greek word kurios *in verse six. If Jesus willed it, the centurion knew He could speak the word and his servant would be healed. But if not, that was His business. He had the authority to command life. If he did not choose to heal his servant, then the centurion would not dispute it, for Jesus alone had the authority to give life to whom He chose.*

This, then, is faith, the sort of faith that impressed Jesus: the recognition that we are not gods with authority over our own lives (indeed, we have already proved ourselves unworthy of that authority), coupled with the recognition that in fact Jesus Christ is Lord, and that He alone holds proper authority over our lives.

Note that the proof of that faith will become evident as our attention and concern is weaned away from ourselves and we come to share Christ's compassion and concern for the world.

CHAPTER FIVE

Honest Doubt

Thomas
(John 20:24–31)

I love Thomas!

We don't know nearly as much about him as we do about some other disciples, but what I *do* know impresses me. He's the sort of straightforward, fearlessly honest person every group needs to keep it from hypocrisy and careless judgment.

Thomas' name, in both Aramaic and Hebrew, means "twin," making John's regular appellation "Thomas (called Didymus)"—the Greek word for "twin"—somewhat redundant. What it suggests is that this was more of a nickname than anything else. Everyone simply knew him as "the Twin." Most later works refer to him as Judas Thomas, and if Judas was his given name, it is not surprising that the group dropped it entirely. They already had two Judases to keep track of among the twelve. (I sometimes wonder if Thomas' twin, whoever he or she was, approved of his going off and following some itinerant teacher. If he or she shared Thomas' natural skepticism, some serious doubts about what Thomas was doing would have been raised, too!)

We, of course, have given him our own nickname. We call him "Doubting Thomas," a disparaging epithet that I think is unfortunate—if not unfair. It's probably too late to change what has become a common metaphor in our language, but I would like to suggest that it would be kinder and perhaps more accurate to refer to this sometimes maligned disciple as "Honest Thomas."

John, I believe, admired his colleague's honesty. He quotes Thomas on four crucial occasions when his observations had a particularly significant effect, and climaxes his gospel with Thomas's magnificent confession of faith recorded in John 20:28. The first quotation we hear from John comes near the end of Jesus' ministry when the Master's popularity had waned as the authorities placed more and more pressure on Him. Many erstwhile followers had fallen away. The last time they had been in Jerusalem before the fateful Passion Week, the opposition had turned particularly hostile with several attempts to seize Jesus and stone Him. The group had barely escaped with their lives and had retreated to a safer part of the country, across the Jordan River from Jericho.

But then came word that Jesus' good friend Lazarus was critically ill. The disciples just knew Jesus would be tempted to go back to heal him, but they knew as well that if He did, their lives would be in jeopardy. So when Jesus suggested that they accompany Him back to Judea (in John, chapter 11), the disciples were clearly reluctant to go. "'But Rabbi,' they said, 'a short while ago the Jews tried to stone you, and yet you are going back there?'" When Jesus tried to reassure them, they countered with their own hopeful assurance that Lazarus was likely to get better on his own. Just leave him alone; he'll sleep it off.

When Jesus reveals that in fact Lazarus has already died and that He is going back in any case, it is Thomas who steps forward, for the first time in the gospels, with the challenge that they need to accompany Jesus even if it means their own death—and he clearly supposes that it will!

Here we see the size of Thomas' heart and the depth of his commitment, albeit expressed in a rather pessimistic observation. He does not want Jesus to die alone, and his faithfulness and courage move him to do what he believes is right regardless of the cost. We are shown his respect for Jesus, as well as his realistic assessment of the profound importance of Jesus' life and teachings, as Thomas makes a decision many later believers have had to make as well. The issues are clear in his mind and he decides at that moment that he would choose death *with* Jesus rather than life *without* Him. Thomas' straightforward, honest courage enables him to look even Death in the eye and proceed regardless of the cost or the consequences. His honesty either persuades or shames the others into accompanying Jesus as well.

The next time we hear from Thomas is in the midst of the most significant and intense discussion Jesus ever had with His disciples. It is at the Last Supper on the eve of His own death, and Jesus is telling them that He is "going away" and they will not be able to accompany Him. This is, as you can imagine, devastating news for these men who had given up everything in order to be with Him. They protest vociferously, and Jesus tries to calm them by asking them to trust Him ("Do you believe in God? Believe also in me.") and reassuring them that at some time in the future they will be able to follow Him.

Nobody has a clue what He is talking about, of course, but no one wants to admit it—you know how we often try to keep a conversation going and not appear too stupid while we try to figure out what in the world the person is talking about.

But it is Thomas again, with his straightforward, non-apologetic honesty who finally says, "Lord, I am drawing a blank here! I don't know what you're talking about! You tell us we know the way to the place where you are going, but we don't even know where you are going, so how in the world can we know the way?"

The question triggers one of the most powerful statements of Jesus' identity and mission. Keep in mind it is in response to Thomas' willingness to admit his ignorance! (I don't know about you, but I often have a difficult time admitting my ignorance. Nevertheless it is a great way to learn.) Thomas says, "I don't know what you're talking about. Will you explain it?" and Jesus did.

This, then, is the Thomas we encounter in John 20. Honest almost to a fault, with the courage to take unpopular stands, not caring a fig about his image, far too rigorous and individual a thinker to ever be "politically correct."

Don't you just love the people Jesus chose to follow Him? It must have been a delight for Him to watch their character emerge. He knew that what some people saw as exasperating skepticism in Thomas was in fact a simple integrity. So I rather imagine that Jesus was not surprised nor was He disappointed in the reaction for which Thomas has become so well known to history.

As John comes to the climax of his account, Jesus has been crucified and His scattered followers are disillusioned and fearful. Thomas has gone off somewhere, perhaps to grieve alone, and the others are in hiding. But then, in an absolutely unprecedented and completely unanticipated development, Jesus begins to appear first to one, and then to another, and finally to the whole group of disciples, *sans* Thomas. At least that is what they report to him when he returns.

But Thomas greets their wild stories with blank incredulity. "I'm sorry, that simply cannot be, no matter what these intelligent and well-meaning people say. I mean, people don't just rise from the dead!" They had seen him nailed to the cross. They had seen the soldier thrust his spear through Jesus' heart, for God's sake! It was impossible! Whatever they thought they had seen, Thomas could not accept so preposterous and unlikely an explanation. These things just didn't happen! When a person was dead, he was dead! In his estimation they had been too quick to accept what they *wanted* to be true. They wanted Jesus to be alive again. They wanted it desperately. And therefore they had been too quick to accept this explanation. He did not doubt they *thought* they had seen Jesus alive again (they were honest men and women after all), but undoubtedly they had not *really* examined all the evidence and considered all the alternatives. This would not be the first time he would have to be the one to ask the hard questions and maybe get the others to accept the bitter truth. "Unless I see the nail marks in his hands and put my finger where the nails were, and put my hand into his side, I will not believe it," Thomas says.

What we see here is a thoroughly consistent picture of Thomas. He would not say that he believed something he didn't believe, any more than he would say that he understood something he did not understand. As William Barclay observes, Thomas would never still his doubts by pretending they did not exist. He is uncompromisingly honest, a man who insists on asking all the tough questions and facing up to the truth no matter how difficult it is to accept. We sometimes get irritated with such people, but without them most of us are far too easily led astray. So Thomas throws a wet blanket on their celebration with his skeptic's instinct to distrust the answer everybody most wants to hear.

To their credit, the other disciples let him nurse his honest doubt. They did not feel compelled to condemn him or ridicule his doubts. We are the ones who started calling him "Doubting Thomas." They did not begin to shun him or exclude him from their fellowship. They did not even attempt to argue him into submission. Faith does not need to resort to any of these alternatives. Genuine faith is compelling precisely because it does not become hysterical or coercive. The Inquisition was motivated by fear, not by faith. Fear tries to reinforce a weak position by quelling dissent or forcing conformity. It is the motivation behind the cowardly phenomenon of "politically correct" thinking today, which is far too lacking in confidence to tolerate dissent. We can't consider another position because we are too worried about the vulnerability of our own.

But faith, genuine conviction, rests easily on those who hold it, for they believe that Truth must ultimately win its own converts. True believers simply live consistently, speaking boldly and without apology, for they know that all honest thinkers will eventually be drawn to the truth, and those who refuse to deal honestly with the truth would not be convinced by arguments no matter how persuasive, nor humbled by any pressure to conform. So the other disciples shrug off Thomas' refusal to believe and just continue to love him and include him, at the same time never backing away from their own convictions.

A week later, Jesus appears again, His specific mission being to convince Thomas with tangible evidence. After greeting them all, Jesus turns to Thomas and says, "Put your finger here; see my hands. Reach out your hand and put it into my side." Thomas looks at Him and apparently doesn't move. Jesus says, "Stop doubting and believe." He is saying, there is a time to doubt, Thomas, but there is also a time to believe. Don't ever let your honest skepticism turn into a specious cynicism that will not accept anything. Here is the evidence you have been asking for. If you are as honest a man as I take you for, you will accept verification as courageously as you accept falsification. There are cynics who take the easy and thoughtless road of rejecting everything, and they are no more praiseworthy than the thoughtless dupe or fool who accepts everything.

Thomas' doubts were not excuses, they did not imply a lack of commitment. How many times have we hidden behind our doubts or our questions simply because we were afraid to make a commitment? Thomas was not that way. His doubts were genuine questions honestly considered. We know this because the instant his questions were answered, he responded with the most candid and powerful expression of faith in all of the gospels. Going beyond anything expressed by any other witness to date, Thomas looked at Jesus and exclaimed, "My Lord and my God!" No one had ever said that about Jesus before.

You see, for Thomas the whole thing fit together in an instant because he had been asking the right questions and honestly seeking the answers. He was not hiding behind his questions; he was honestly seeking the answers. He was unwilling to embrace the faith just because it was what he *wanted* to believe, but he was quite willing to embrace the Truth with his whole heart, regardless of the consequences, once his honest doubts had been addressed. Thomas doubted, not because he was afraid of commitment, but because he wanted to be certain of what he committed himself to. And the result was that his faith became more confident and resilient, precisely because he had been willing to go through this uncompromising examination.

Hear me! Honest doubt does not jeopardize faith. Honest doubt strengthens faith! Tradition credits Thomas with establishing the church in India. Apparently his honest faith became a compelling testimony that continues to bear fruit to this day.

Here then is the ultimate test of Thomas' honesty. *Once he was sure of the truth, he was willing to submit to it without reservation.* This should certainly be the challenge to us. If Jesus was God, then He must also be Thomas' Lord. It cannot be both ways. We cannot say Jesus is God, but He is not going to be my Lord. That is the road to death. This was not a trivial intellectual exercise to establish some theoretical truth or disestablish some rival philosophy. This was a deep and vital and ultimately personal search for the Truth to which one must submit if one is ever to know life and joy and fulfillment and power. True truth is not ultimately an intellectual concept to which we give mental assent. It is a sovereign Lord before whom we must bow. And honest Thomas was willing to do just that.

For this reason, Jesus does not condemn Thomas for his honest doubts, even though He points out that not everyone will have access to the sort of proofs Thomas required. Some, including us, would have to believe on less tangible evidence. But Jesus would not leave them without evidence. In fact, the reason John included this account here is because Thomas' conversion is among the most convincing bits of evidence we have. We know this man was not gullible, as we might suspect of anyone who comes up with the preposterous notion that a man who was crucified could rise from the dead. We know that one of the most powerful testimonies to the deity of Jesus Christ came from one of the most reluctant witnesses—the man who was always willing to ask the toughest questions and face the harshest implications, who was unwilling to be convinced without the most compelling and undeniable evidence. I'm glad Thomas was on the scene. His very skepticism becomes for us a source of assurance for our own faith in Jesus Christ, since we were not there.

There is a final word of encouragement for those of us who follow Thomas to faith in Jesus. "Because you have seen me, you have believed"; Jesus observed to this worthy skeptic, "[but] blessed are those who have not seen and yet have believed."

This is an interesting statement. We have been considering the value of doubt and Jesus' respect for honest questions. This statement may seem to contradict that. But I believe that Jesus is not saying He extends greater honor to those who believe without asking the tough questions. That could not be, for those who refuse to seek answers to honest questions are not full of faith, they are just careless, and far too likely to be led astray.

Rather I believe Jesus is pointing out something quite different. Jesus' emphasis here is on the blessing that He offers, and "blessings" *always* come from trusting God. This is a simple, natural, and inevitable fact. It just takes place. Like nourishment comes from eating healthy food, blessing comes from trusting God. Therefore, whatever it takes to get you to believe and trust in Him *will* bring you His blessing. That is a certainty. Now it is true that the longer you remain in your disbelief, the longer you deprive yourself of His blessing.

Not everyone will have access to, and not everyone will require the sort of proof Thomas required. Yet whatever ultimately brings them to faith will also bring them God's marvelous blessing. "Blessed are those who have not seen and yet have believed." That is simply a promise of blessing for believers, whether they were on the scene or not.

John concludes his whole gospel with the observation that he has shared all this, including, perhaps specifically, the account of Thomas' conversion from skepticism to belief so that you and I may also come to belief. He says in that final sentence "that by believing you may have life in his name."

Do you have doubts or questions about Jesus' life or death or resurrection? Let me encourage you to be as honest in addressing them as Thomas was, and as courageous in embracing Jesus Christ as Lord when He has answered your questions.

The Crooked-Hearted Man

Simon Magus
(Acts 8:9–24)

Simon, a dabbler in the occult, was a fascination to the people of Samaria. Some might have called their curiosity an obsession. He liked it that way. Very quickly, he learned how much power and influence these skills brought.

He may have begun with relatively harmless ritual incantations and attempts to predict the future, but he soon learned that he would need to demonstrate some results if he were to maintain any real degree of influence over the populace, something he wanted desperately to do. The way to do that, he determined, was to get in touch with the world of the spirits that might invisibly affect the material world. And what perhaps surprised Simon in the beginning was the relative ease with which he was able to do that.

There have always been skeptics who believe the spirit world does not exist and that only the material world we perceive with our five senses is real. But of course this error is made immediately obvious by our perception of ourselves as essentially spiritual beings. This living, self-conscious force that animates our bodies is experienced as contiguous with and yet separate from the body that is its home. Although every cell of the body is still present at the moment of death, we have an immediate sense of emptiness, the recognition that the person or the spirit that inhabited that body is now gone. Thus we are quite aware of the reality of the spirit world from our own perception of ourselves as spirits.

Another argument for the existence of the spirit world is our Christian reliance on prayer as a central aspect of our faith. In prayer we find ourselves in touch with God and perhaps with a larger body of spiritual forces. The existence of angels is assumed throughout the Scriptures; they are specifically described as spiritual agents who minister to our needs at God's bidding.

Thus it is no surprise to find abundant reference on the pages of both history and scripture to spiritual forces. Not all of them are good, of course. Many of them, according to the Scriptures, have detached themselves from God by rebellion against His authority. Still, they, too, are active in our world, but forces for ill rather than for good.

In any case, Simon apparently made a fine living, and— more importantly to him—maintained a powerful influence over his countrymen by consulting these spirits and perhaps by manipulating the occult spiritual forces, as many before him had done successfully. He amazed people with his sorcery and was happy to be perceived by them as someone great—some-one in touch with the Force, the Great Power.

However, one day a young evangelist by the name of Philip arrived in town. Philip was a new and articulate Christian who had been commissioned by the church in Jerusalem to share the incredibly good news about Jesus' death and resurrection. Because of the persecution in Jerusalem, Philip had come to Samaria.

The power of God's Spirit was upon him, and he was tremendously successful, both in articulating this new faith and in demonstrating its power. Like his Master, Jesus, Philip was able to cast evil spirits out of people, as well as to heal them of paralysis and various crippling or debilitating diseases.

What was perhaps most impressive about Philip was that he did not try to manipulate people by cultivating an aura of mystery and dark power over which he alone exercised control. Instead, Philip was very transparent, very straightforward. He proclaimed quite openly that the power he exercised came from the God who had created the universe, and that this power was available to all the people to accomplish good things, to bring about transformation in their own lives.

Simon recognized the superiority of this Power over his own and stood in awe of Philip. When the young evangelist invited people to be baptized and place their faith in Jesus Christ, Simon did so, clearly moved by the dramatic power of the Spirit at work in Philip. In fact, Simon became so obsessed with Philip and his humble, genuine power and influence that he began to follow him everywhere he went.

Simon had received Christian baptism and professed faith in Jesus Christ, but we are not convinced this was more than a superficial conversion. He seemed not to have grasped the point of the Gospel, and our clue is the way in which he is still enamored with power and with the spectacular. Quite clearly what impressed him was the power Philip exhibited and the influence it gave him over people's lives. It was an attractive temptation to Simon. As we soon learn, even though Simon had professed faith in Christ, and even though he no doubt sincerely believed, nevertheless his heart was not yet right with God.

What happened next intrigued Simon even more. To understand it we need to understand the historical tension between the Samaritans and the Jews. Way back in the eighth century B.C. the Assyrians had conquered the Northern Kingdom of Israel whose capital was in Samaria. The majority of the Jews were carried away captive and resettled in other countries within the Assyrian Empire. At the same time, displaced persons from other conquered countries were transplanted into Samaria. In time, the Jews who remained intermarried with these foreigners, producing the mixed Samaritan race.

Jews from the Southern Kingdom of Judah, however, who were defeated by the Babylonians about 150 years later, fiercely resisted being absorbed by other races as their kinsmen had been, and eventually returned to Israel under Ezra and Nehemiah. You may recall reading those passages from the Old Testament in which we find the long genealogies recorded upon the people's return. They were trying to trace their heritage in order to prove that they had not lost the purity of the Jewish race during their time in captivity. To them, the mixed northern peoples were anathema, the product of a humiliating compromise they themselves had resisted. So the Jews had a difficult time with the Samaritans, and always looked upon them with contempt.

When lives began to be transformed by the power of the Holy Spirit, however, following Jesus' death and resurrection, the earliest Christians quite spontaneously set aside this long history of racial prejudice and began to share the good news even with the Samaritans, as Jesus had challenged them. Clearly the gospel was taking root in their lives and old prejudices were being overcome.

When Philip's evangelistic mission met with such remarkable success here in Samaria, leading many to believe in Jesus, the apostles in Jerusalem sent Peter and John, Jesus' two closest friends, to confirm that God's Spirit was indeed bringing new life even to the Samaritans. When they laid their hands on the new believers in a symbolic gesture indicating that God's

Spirit was being passed along from Jesus to His disciples and from them to these believers as well, something spectacular happened.

We are not told exactly what it was. Perhaps the people spoke in other languages as they had initially on the day of Pentecost in Jerusalem. Perhaps there was some other astonishing sign of God's presence. Whatever it was, God wanted to show that Pentecost applied to the Samaritans as well as the Jews—those old barriers were beginning to break down as God's Spirit drew men and women, Jew and gentile, slave and free into His kingdom.

Simon was impressed! Whatever the evidence of God's Spirit, he was impressed with what took place when Peter and John laid hands on these individuals. Captivated by the dramatic and spectacular aspects of Christianity, and, I am afraid, still failing to grasp the heart of the gospel, he immediately saw the potential for personal advantage in this phenomenon. Think about it! What influence one could have over others if one held this power to affect lives so profoundly! If he could just get Peter and John to share this strategic power with him! Think what prestige it would give him! Think what power it would give him over the lives of others!

The sin of Simon anticipated a host of modern "Christians" who look for some personal advantage in the things of the Spirit. Some "faith-healers" seem to have drawn their script directly from this passage. Certainly God's Spirit heals people today. But in the spectacular demonstration of "faith-healing" I think we see the flaw of Simon the sorcerer.

There is tremendous power and potentially significant financial advantage for the person who can, through the laying on of hands and prayer, appear to restore health and wholeness. It is certainly a temptation for TV evangelists to become primarily impressed with themselves and their ability to influence and even control people's lives. And some in the "signs and wonders" community, though they invoke Jesus' name often enough, do not resist this age-old temptation to promote themselves, using their "magic" to draw attention and power. We must not allow God's power to be used for personal power or gain.

Unfortunately, the current church growth movement suffers from a similar temptation—the temptation of success and expanding influence. In some cases, proven marketing techniques manipulated to guarantee well-stocked pews have replaced the irresistible calling of the Holy Spirit. Market niches are carved out; target audiences are selected; felt needs are addressed; seeker-sensitive services are designed; catchy upbeat music is played through the latest high-tech equipment by polished popular performers; laid-back, nonjudgmental, esteem-building eighteen-minute messages are presented; worship and service are made as painless and exciting as possible. It is not that any of these things are bad. The laying on of hands was not bad either. The problem is in our attitude as we approach these things. The problem is in our temptation, like Simon, to manipulate the gospel, or the things of the Spirit, in order to gain some sort of personal advantage or pursue our own agenda.

This principle is so fundamental to the recognition of what it means to be a Christian. The Holy Spirit is not at our service. We are called to be at the Holy Spirit's service. Unfortunately there is an "Aladdin syndrome" at work in churches today. Our prayers too often become an attempt to rub the lamp and have God appear like the genie in the bottle, our wish becoming his command. But—you see—the reverse ought to be true of our prayers—*we* are the servant who appears; it is God's wish that must become our command.

The fact is, as Douglas Webster says in his book, *Selling*

Jesus, not all of these marketing techniques present the Gospel honestly. As he points out,

> The cross [after all] is difficult to market. About the last thing Americans want to hear is a call to self-denial. But Jesus [said], "If any want to become my followers, they must deny themselves and take up their cross and follow me" (Matthew 16:24). We are reluctant to follow Jesus' example. We'd rather base church growth on something that will lure people in and get them involved before we say too much about commitment.[1]

Likewise, Simon was interested in personal advantage, not, self-denial. But as he offered to pay to learn the technique that would allow him power and influence in the church he brought Peter's stern rebuke: "May your money perish with you, because you thought you could buy the gift of God with money!" Actually, I think I owe those who prefer the most literal translation of the original Greek text a slight revision here. If we are translating the Greek with technical accuracy, what Peter said was, "To hell with you and your money!" He really did! He was incensed that anyone would seek personal advantage from the Gospel. He made it clear that the Gospel is not commercial. Profiteering from it would not be tolerated in this new fledgling church. God's Spirit does what He wills, and will not be manipulated by our attempts at power and influence.

We must always remember that we may only be the servants of God's Spirit, never are we His master. We do not control Him. He must control us.

The desire to take personal advantage of the Holy Spirit— to "use" His gifts to gain power and influence or turn the Gospel into a commercial venture from which to seize personal advantage—is to display, as Peter now charges Simon, "a crooked heart." This is the literal meaning of "your heart is not right before God." It is not straight; it is crooked. He had stated his desire to be associated with Jesus, but his heart was still, as verse 23 says, "captive to sin." It was evident in his attitude, in his desire for prestige and power instead of humility and service. There is much speculation in early church history over the subsequent role of Simon Magus. Some say he came to resent Peter for that public humiliation and spent the rest of his life doing all he could to interfere with Peter's ministry. Others say he became the outstanding spokesman for the Gnostic heretics who particularly enjoyed exotic rituals and the power implicit in them. If this is true, then Simon failed at the very point at which his conversion might have become real and genuine. If this is true, he becomes for us a negative example of how we might respond to an encounter with Jesus Christ.

But I will be honest with you. Personally I see none of that here. What I see in the final verse concerning Simon is a genuinely penitent heart, which, if it is true, unquestionably won for him a place in God's kingdom. Grief-stricken and fearful of the consequences of his misplaced expectations—which is most appropriate, ("the fear of the LORD is the beginning of wisdom")—Simon says to Peter, "Pray to the Lord for me so that nothing you have said may happen to me." It is, I believe, this attitude of honest penitence and dependence upon the Lord that alone guarantees for us a place in God's kingdom as well. It is this attitude alone that sets our hearts right with God.

Notes

1 WEBSTER, DOUGLAS D., *Selling Jesus: What's Wrong with Marketing the Church,* (InterVarsity Press, Downers Grove, Illinois, 1992) 20.

That, my sisters and brothers, is fundamentally what the Gospel is all about. I would like to tell you there is great advantage in it for you (indeed I believe there is, especially in an ultimate sense), but God does not call us to personal advantage. He calls us to the cross. He calls us to self-sacrifice and humility. He calls us to place ourselves at His service; and His Spirit will take charge of our lives.

The problem with Simon was really not at all dissimilar to the problem many of us have with the Gospel of Jesus. Our motivation in coming to Christ has altogether too often been entirely self-serving. We are happy to come, to follow, to do this if there is any advantage in it for us.

Too consistently the Gospel is presented as the "answer to all your problems," the guarantee of blessing and safety and prosperity in your life.

And it seems to me that God's response to such a presentation is rather harsh. He says in effect, "To hell with your advantage!" I'm not calling you to advantage. I am not calling you to success. I'm not calling you to personal gain. Understand, I'm not at all pleased with your preoccupation with the exotic effects of the Spirit and the influence that gives you.

Verse 22 points the one route to true discipleship, "Repent of this wickedness and pray to the Lord. Perhaps he will forgive you for having such a thought in your heart." What is required to set our hearts right with the Lord is an acknowledgement of sin and a genuine repentance.

CHAPTER SEVEN

If You Seek Me . . .

Ethiopian Official
(Acts 8:26–39)

A s many years before the time of Christ as we are now after it, the civilization of Egypt was at its peak. The great pyramids had stood for more than five hundred years as symbols of the religious aspirations, aesthetic sophistication, political power and astonishing mathematical and engineering skills of these advanced people, as well as evidence of the spectacular potential of mobilized labor.

By the time of the Middle Kingdom in Egypt, about 2000 B.C., powerful pharaohs who had overseen the flowering of Egyptian literature and art, built temples and sculpture on a colossal scale and inspired a period of breathtaking cultural splendor were pressing southward up the Nile to enlarge their empire. Crossing the first cataract of the Nile at Aswan, they thrust into Nubia, building great forts at strategic narrows such as Buhen and Semna. Eventually they extended their influence through the land known today as the Sudan all the way to the third and fourth cataracts on the Nile, where they would remain in control for another five hundred years.

But eventually the conquered peoples, though deeply influenced by Egyptian beliefs and techniques, threw off Egyptian rule and built the greatest of the old civilizations of inner Africa in the Sudan. The Greeks called these people *aithiops*, which meant "dark-skinned," and referred to the land as Ethiopia, though the land that presently bears that name lies farther south.

By the sixth century B.C., fine masonry towns were spread along the river, graced by extraordinary temples and palaces and pyramids. Ultimately an alphabetic language was developed and original styles in art and architecture flourished.

By the time Greek explorers such as Herodotus had begun to discover Africa, these people, who called themselves Kushites, had an advanced civilization that had developed great ironworks, and began to extend trade to Egypt and Arabia, East Africa, India and perhaps even to China. By the time of Christ this vigorous and advanced culture was sending ambassadors to Rome. The Kushites had accomplished much.

Yet there was at least one man—a very important and influential man—who was not satisfied with the best his culture had produced. The man held a position of great power and influence that had brought him wealth and prestige. He was the chief officer (chamberlain) responsible for the nation's treasury. In this position he answered directly to the queen mother, who bore the dynastic title Candace, and who was responsible for the daily operation of the government—the king being considered too sacred a personage for such functions.

This man—a bit jaded by palace politics—was not impressed with the Kushite lion god with three faces and four arms that eventually displaced the Egyptian-inspired ram god. He had seen enough of the inner circles of power to know that all these hapless gods were cynically manipulated by those in authority to maintain their own power and influence. It seemed to him that some Force, some Power, must supersede all these petty gods who squabbled with each other and rose and fell with the fortunes of their servants.

Commerce with the world beyond the borders of Nubia had allowed him to hear of another God, one who his followers claimed held just such a position of supremacy. This was the God purported to have created the earth and the heavens. This God did not manipulate the laws to favor those in power, as every other god seemed to do. No, this God held all people—kings and peasants, rich and poor, from every tribe and kingdom and nation—accountable for maintaining the same standards of justice and fair play.

This God never hid behind kings and priests, emerging in response to incantations designed to curry His favor. Rather, this God acted boldly and straightforwardly in history to accomplish His own, sometimes mysterious ends. In fact, he had heard rumors that this God had, against all odds, delivered a ragtag group of slaves from his Egyptian forebears.

So many things about this God made sense. He never compromised His moral standards to protect His people or even His own name. At a time in history when nearly all other gods seemed to tolerate or even condone the most outrageous, self-indulgent behavior, this God demanded honesty and consistency and self-discipline from His people. The stories His people told to explain the origin and meaning of life were common sense stories, grounded in history—not the wild and fantastic legends that seemed to characterize every other religion. And the rules this God laid down for His people, unlike anything he found elsewhere, protected the poor and powerless and called the wealthy and powerful to stewardship and accountability.

He didn't know if he could consider this religion to be True in any ultimate sense, but he did know that it provided a world-view that made sense of the things he could observe, and called people to live in a way that seemed fair and right—

indeed, a way that seemed calculated to produce genuine satisfaction and joy.

So the man began to study the sacred writings of these people who were called the Jews, and seized the opportunity to travel to Jerusalem to participate in the worship of their God, Yahweh. The extent of his worship there in Jerusalem is unknown, since one requirement of his office was that he become a eunuch. Earlier on this would have disqualified him from some levels of participation in worship, though the laws were changing. Such regulations were of no great concern to him, however. He was not trying to defend himself; he was on a quest to know the Truth, and was willing to take the initiative to search for it wherever it might be found and whatever the personal cost. Although this man could not have anticipated it, God was about to honor his honest search. He had been to Jerusalem and had begun the long journey by carriage back to the south through Palestine, swinging west to the coast past the Sinai desert on his way to Egypt. From there he could continue the thousand-mile journey to his home by boat. Along the way he would use his time studying the Hebrew Scriptures, searching for that Truth for which his heart longed.

Meanwhile, God had recently raised up a remarkable young Jewish-Christian evangelist named Philip. We know little about Philip, a man who apparently grasped the heart of the Gospel long before most of his associates.

It would take the brilliant apostle Paul much longer to get to this same place, but he would eventually write to the churches in Galatia that "in Christ Jesus you are all [children] of God, through faith. . . . There is neither Jew nor Greek, there is neither slave nor free, there is neither male nor female; for you are all one in Christ Jesus." That was a difficult realization for Paul, who as an educated Jew, a free Roman citizen, and a male enjoyed all the positions of privilege in his society.

But Philip had a refreshing spirit and an open and liberal

mind. He seemed to have immediately recognized that all barriers were broken down in Jesus Christ, and he had a special place in his heart for Gentiles, outcasts and even women.

Philip was a man recognized for his wisdom and spirituality, and as a result was among the seven selected by the church in Jerusalem and commissioned through the laying on of hands to oversee their ministry of compassion to people in severe economic need. That is where Philip's ministry had begun.

When his colleague, Stephen, was killed and he was forced to leave the city, he went immediately to Samaria, of all places, where he began preaching the Gospel to the outcasts of his day. (This would be somewhat like Mother Teresa's ministry to the lowest of the low in Calcutta, searching out the people who have the least privilege and ministering to them.) The half-breed Samaritans were scornfully excluded from Jewish worship. They were about the only peoples who were not even allowed to become proselytes. But that didn't keep Philip from establishing a highly successful mission there, which even astonished the apostles.

And Philip's home must have been an interesting one. Later on four of Philip's daughters would become Spirit-filled preachers of the Word, a phenomenon that would have shocked the early church, even though the prophet Joel had predicted that in the last days God's Spirit would allow both sons and daughters to prophesy. God was confident that in Philip He had the man who would not hesitate to bring the compassion of Jesus Christ to a man who was not only another color, but a sexual anomaly as well. He knew that God's Spirit transcended economic barriers, racial-ethnic barriers, barriers of creed, color, and gender.

So, through God's providence, these two remarkable men—the honest seeker and the open-hearted evangelist—met. God's Spirit sent Philip down to the desert road that leads southwest from Jerusalem to Gaza. Along the road he encountered the Nubian chamberlain sitting in his carriage, reading from a scroll of the prophet Isaiah. Ancient manuscripts, more than modern phonetic writing, were difficult to read if one did not read them aloud, so as Philip approached, he heard the man reading the incredible account of the Suffering Servant from the prophet Isaiah. You know it—it is from the fifty-third chapter:

> He was wounded for our transgressions, he was bruised for our iniquities; upon him was the chastisement that made us whole, and with his stripes we are healed. All we like sheep have gone astray; we have turned every one to his own way; and the LORD has laid on him the iniquity of us all.
>
> He was led like a sheep to the slaughter, and as a lamb before the shearer is silent, so he did not open his mouth. In his humiliation, he was deprived of justice. Who can speak of his descendants? For his life was taken from the earth.[1]

Before the New Testament was written there could not have been another passage in all of Scripture that would give a clearer account of the Gospel of Jesus Christ. There could not be another passage in all the Old Testament that would give a more precise account of what God was accomplishing through the death and resurrection of Jesus than this section of Isaiah 53! It could hardly be a coincidence that the Ethiopian treasurer was reading from this very passage as Philip approached!

Philip asked him, "Do you understand what you are reading?" It's a perfect opening. There is no threat, no condescension, no unwelcome intrusion into the man's privacy, only a question that allows the man to make a choice about whether he is willing to explore this issue further. And because he is an honest seeker, the official *is* willing to explore it further. He replies, "How can I unless someone explains it to me?" and proceeds to invite Philip to join him in the chariot to talk further.

Acknowledging Philip as someone familiar with the passages, he asked, "Tell me, please, who is the prophet talking about, himself or someone else?" And Philip then, having been invited to share his faith and understanding, had the opportunity to respond to the chamberlain's searching questions as the cart jogged along the dusty roadway.

His precise words are not recorded here, but we are told that beginning with that very passage of Scripture, Philip told him the good news about Jesus. No doubt he took some time to establish Jesus' identity and tell something about his life, his miracles, and his teaching. I am certain when he came to the account of the crucifixion, he pointed out that Jesus' suffering was for us—that he was paying the penalty for our sins when he hung wounded and bruised from the cross, as Isaiah says, for God had "laid on him the iniquity of us all." I imagine he explained how Jesus had been humiliated and deprived of justice, as Isaiah had predicted, and then of how his life was taken literally from the earth, as he was first crucified, then raised from the dead, and finally ascended to the right hand of God.

To all this the Queen's treasurer listened with rapt attention, as little by little the pieces of his long and diligent search began to fall into place. Here was the explanation of it all. What an awesome thing for the God who created the universe to visit His people here! But how would we have ever come to know Him if He did not reveal himself? What a truly astonishing thing that this God, unlike any other god in history, would deign to soil himself with the sins of His children and ultimately die for them! What God would do such a thing? But then how else could He maintain holiness and justice while still preserving a fallen and sinful race? This God had compassion like no other God of whom he had ever heard. His creative and overwhelming method of dealing with sin and righteousness seemed logical and consistent. This had to be the Truth for which he had been seeking all his life. So what would it take for him, a world-class sinner but sincere seeker, to embrace this remarkable religion?

No fear, I expect Philip explained, if your heart is in the right place you will not need to embrace Him—He will embrace you! Perhaps he followed the model of Peter's Pentecost sermon: "Repent and be baptized . . . in the name of Jesus Christ for the forgiveness of your sins. And you will receive the gift of the Holy Spirit."

In any case, when the official grasped Philip's explanation, the whole thing made sense to him. Here was a "real" religion that dealt with the "real" issues a thoughtful or sensitive person struggled with every day. Here was a faith that took seriously the holiness of God and yet offered hope to a sinful and broken humanity. This was what he had been looking for all his life! The God he had known intuitively must underlie all reality; this God had touched the earth in the person of Jesus, revealing himself in all His glory, grace and truth.

"Look, here is water," the dark-skinned chamberlain pointed out as they approached one of the springs along the roadway. "Why shouldn't I be baptized?" And Philip, with a few questions assuring himself of the man's genuine penitence and faith, climbed down from the carriage with him to perform the ritual that would mark this man a true son of the Living God— not a seeker any longer.

His task complete, the Spirit summoned Philip to the coastal cities where his fruitful ministry would continue to grow and expand. But the chief officer of the Kushite treasury continued on his way rejoicing, we are told, for his long search had finally borne its fruit, and he found his yearning spirit content with the Truth as he set his sights toward home.

Ever since Jesus made His claim to be "the Way, the Truth, and the Life," explaining that no one could come to the Father except by Him, and Peter announced that "salvation is found in no one else, for there is no other name under heaven given to men by which we must be saved," people have wondered what happens to sincere and honest people who have no opportunity to hear the gospel. And while the Scriptures never address the question directly, it seems to me that the experience of the Ethiopian eunuch, as we have known him, might give us a clue. For here was a man who honestly desired to know the truth. Here was a man who was willing to make an effort to search for that truth. Here was a man who was ready to embrace that truth if he found it. And God rewarded that honesty, and that effort, and that search.

Once before, to a lost and rebellious people, God had said through the prophet Jeremiah that if they would call upon Him and pray to Him, He would hear them. "You will seek me and find me;" He had said, "when you seek me with all your heart, I will be found by you." That was the promise.

This man may not have known the promise, but it applied to him nonetheless, and as he honestly searched for God, the promise was a guarantee that his search would be rewarded. Philip, of course, had an indispensable role in the fulfillment of that promise. Had he not been willing to be used by God's Spirit, the man could not have heard.

Believers today are called to testify to the grace of our Lord Jesus Christ, to go into all lands and nations to give honest seekers the opportunity to hear. Those who know Christ may well be the means by which God responds to honest searchers. But in response to our concern, we are assured here that as God looks upon the heart, those who have a truly penitent spirit will have opportunity to find Him.

God has always been in the business of evaluating a person's heart. It is not so much that a person has stumbled on the right words to say, the right formula for salvation. Rather the LORD looks upon the heart. He forgives those who humble themselves before Him, and rewards those who honestly seek Him. There is no indication anywhere in the scriptures that God would refuse to forgive those who genuinely humble themselves before Him, or that He would refuse to honor an honest search.

This issue of an honest search for the truth is equally relevant for each of us today. If we spend our time complaining about God's fairness, or ignoring the opportunities He gives to come to know Him, we have no one to blame but ourselves.

Do you truly desire to know Him? Are you willing to discipline yourself to search honestly to know the Truth? Are you willing to commit yourself without reservation to the Truth when you find it? These are the prerequisites for a successful search. But you may rest assured, God will not hide from the honest seeker.

Notes

1 Isaiah 53:5–6 from Hebrew translation; 7–8 from Greek translation.

The Heart of a Revolution

Saul
(Acts 9:1–22)

The door of Caiaphas' office burst open. In strode a man in his early thirties, short, stocky, prematurely balding, with a dark beard and a look of fierce determination on his face. Caiaphas' surprise turned to quiet amusement as he recognized his stormy visitor. "Saul, what a pleasant surprise," he said, honestly enough. "Do come in!" he added—unnecessarily.

"I need to talk with you immediately," Saul said abruptly. Caiaphas crossed the room, motioning Saul to a seat. He appreciated Saul's energy and sense of moral urgency, but it was important to keep it channeled against the proper enemies. (One of his jobs, as he saw it, was to take bright, articulate, self-assured young zealots like Saul and use their fire and passion to maintain his *own* position and power as high priest. "It is for the good of the temple and the people," he assured himself.)

Caiaphas himself sat down, but Saul continued to storm about the office. "I want letters of extradition to the synagogues in Damascus," he demanded. "I thought those damnable followers of 'The Way' would back off after Stephen was put to death, but if anything they have gotten even more bold and persistent. If we don't stop them now there is no telling how much damage they will do. Now I hear they're getting a foothold in Damascus. If they go unchallenged there, this foolishness will spread along the caravan routes into northern Syria, Mesopotamia, Anatolia, Persia and Arabia; there is no telling where it will stop. You know how ready people are to accept any challenge to established authority. This is no time for tolerance. Give me some men and the authority of the Sanhedrin and I'll arrest anyone I find and bring them back here to face trial. If we can't get them to publicly renounce their faith, we'll imprison them. We'll put them to death if necessary!"

Caiaphas looked approvingly at the intense, fiery young man before him. He was glad to have Saul on his side—and he would readily concede the man was dangerous. For one thing, he was brilliant, an intellectual of the first order, articulate and terribly persuasive. For another, he seemed to be a man of boundless energy and almost reckless courage. When you put that together with his cosmopolitan background and his impeccable credentials, you definitely had a winner.

Paul had been born in the Cilician city of Tarsus, a center of Greek culture and commerce. His parents, however, were devout Jews who had sent him to Jerusalem to study under the great rabbi, Gamalial—like having a degree from Oxford or Harvard today. And if his Greek language and logic and his Hebrew learning were not enough, he had the additional and rare privilege of Roman citizenship, which allowed him uncommon access to people and places of influence as well as extraordinary protection.

"You're right, Saul. They're peasants, uneducated plebeians, vulgar anarchists who would stop at nothing to overthrow the established order. They pretend to be 'religious' but you and I know they are nothing more than opportunists, quick to recruit a following in a cynical bid to advance their own agenda. You never met this Jesus whom they claim to serve, but let me assure you, he was trouble from the start—from Nazareth, of all places, without a stitch of formal education. I'll admit he had a charismatic personality, which is the only reason he survived as long as he did, but no thinking person, Saul, would take him seriously."

It was true, Saul had never actually met Jesus. And that troubled him a bit in his more thoughtful moments. He hated rejecting something without actually having some firsthand experience with it. But he knew enough about "the Way" to know that it went contrary to virtually all contemporary thinking. And, after all, the kinds of people who were drawn to it were certainly not the sort of people Saul wanted to be identified with. They were becoming the butt of many jokes in the intellectual community, and it would have been professional suicide to try to defend their absurd theory of a crucified Messiah.

The more Saul thought about it, the angrier he became. Who were these people to challenge the entire world view of both the religious and the intellectual community? He was offended by their lack of respect for his discipline and his lifetime of orthodox learning. How could they be right and everybody else be wrong? The arrogance of such a conclusion was so intellectually and personally offensive that he dismissed his doubts about the unassailability of his own position, dismissed as well his reluctant admission that he had never really examined the new beliefs for himself. These people had to be stopped, that was all there was to it. They could corrupt the minds of a whole generation if they were not simply cut off from the public debate as quickly as possible.

"Get me the letters, and I'll get you these lackwitted

Sophists," Saul replied. Caiaphas smiled sardonically and reached for his pen.

It is very important to recognize that Saul was typical of so many among the "educated elite" who prejudge Christianity without actually examining it on its own merits. They have already accepted a "system," and Christianity doesn't fit into that system, so obviously it cannot be true. It is not that Christianity has been tried and found wanting. As others have pointed out, it has been found demanding and never tried! It has been rejected without a fair trial. It has been dismissed without honest and responsibly critical consideration.

Furthermore, I think there is a prejudice, a tendency to "look down on" those who accept Christianity. Because the Christian position has been rejected as unintellectual in advance, anyone who accepts it is automatically labeled gullible and incapable of critical thinking. This convenient epithet allows the pseudointellectual to dismiss Christianity without ever examining it. One need never be honestly challenged by its troubling truths. The denigration of "the Way" continues today.

Frankly, it is quite understandable that people don't like to consider Christianity seriously. You know the reason why: implicit in the teachings of Jesus Christ is a non-negotiable claim on your life. If you wish never to be placed in the position of having to face such a claim, you might simply try to avoid it in advance, and the belittling of Christianity very conveniently does that.

Of course, such a position is hardly defensible for those who would like us to believe that they are truly "liberal" thinkers and rigorous intellectual explorers. It is always possible, after all, that an honest examination would prove Christianity credible. But for defenders of any age's politically correct thinking, such a conclusion would be potentially disastrous! It would make them appear foolish to their intellectual colleagues. Worse, it might demand that they totally redirect their lives. An honest consideration of the Christian faith is precluded by those who think in this way.

Fortunately for the future of the Christian faith, Saul ultimately proved to be both more *honest* and more *courageous* than the pseudointellectuals of his day. It took a remarkable experience that shook him considerably; but the real test of his character and courage would lie in his response.

One hundred forty miles of rugged terrain and desert lie between Jerusalem and Damascus—a week's journey on foot or by horse. What Saul thought about during the journey is not recorded for us. Whether, during the long nights as he slept on the rocky ground he saw the face of Stephen, in whose death by stoning he had participated, and wondered what would motivate a man to give up his life for an apparently lost cause, we are not told. If he ever questioned the integrity of his tirade against the early believers, he kept it to himself.

Perhaps the pervasive approval of a self-satisfied society served to reinforce his stubborn convictions. It is comfortable, if not particularly healthy, to have the support of the community even in a lie. Whatever his thoughts, he seemed unprepared for the encounter that welcomed him to the outskirts of the ancient city of Damascus.

About midday, Paul tells us later, as they approached the luxuriant gardens and groves of the city, looming like a fanciful mirage in the midst of the barren wilderness of sand and rock through which they had been traveling, suddenly a light brighter than the sun blazed around him and his companions. Blinded by the light, Saul fell to the ground, but not before he had glimpsed a personal presence in the supernatural brilliance around him. Then a voice rang in his ears, speaking in his native tongue, "Saul, Saul, why do you persecute me?"

Saul was terrified, as any sane person would be. He was a Jew, after all, and this was like the shekinah glory that his ancestors had seen in the wilderness. It was like the presence of God on Mt. Sinai, from which his people shrank in terror. "Who are you, Lord?" Saul asked, no doubt covering his head.

"I am Jesus, whom you are persecuting," the voice replied. "Now get up and go into the city, and you will be told what you must do."

You and I may speculate about ecstatic visions, but there was no doubt in Saul's mind that he was in the actual presence of Jesus Christ. That reality utterly transformed his thinking from that moment forward. I think you would know if God actually spoke to you. And the fact is, the whole experience turned Saul's airtight system on its ear. Nothing else about the relative logic or irrationality of the Christian faith had changed. The whole Christian world and life view remained precisely what it had been when he had previously rejected it out of hand. There was no new knowledge about the Christian faith. But Saul had encountered the Living Christ, and in that moment of encounter with the Living Christ everything changed.

If Jesus was dead, as Saul had been led to believe, then the whole Christian system was a deception worth every ounce of his hostile counteraction. But if Jesus were actually alive— risen from the dead and ascended to the right hand of God— then quite frankly everything in the Christian faith made perfectly logical sense. It was not contradicted by any known fact or logical deduction whatsoever, no matter what the intellectual community might have thought. In that moment, with the light still blinding his eyes, and the voice still ringing in his ears, Saul realized that in fact Jesus *was* alive.

Saul was stunned. He had encountered Jesus and now everything he had thought, everything he had believed, was turned upside down. Could it possibly be that he and all those he knew who were so self-righteously confident of their position were wrong? The voice had told him to get up and go into the city where he would be told what he must do next. Saul could not resist. He struggled to his feet, digging his fists into his eyes, which still felt the pain of the blinding light. But when he opened his eyes he could see nothing.

His companions, who had witnessed the sound and the light, but had not heard a distinguishable voice or sensed the presence of the Lord, knew something spectacular had happened and concluded that it must have been a thunderbolt.

In a way it was. A millennium and a half later a near miss from a bolt of lightning would change the way Martin Luther looked at life. A lot of people are shaken to their senses by a close brush with mortality that motivates them to consider once-rejected beliefs about life and death more seriously.

For Saul, the effect was similar, but this was a close encounter of a much more personal kind. He had thought Jesus dead, and the accounts of His resurrection a deception. But now he had met Him. The reality of this encounter was increasingly confirmed through further experiences in the days ahead. His friends, Paul tells us, led him into the city where for three days he remained blind and so traumatized that he neither ate nor drank anything. During this time he saw a vision of a man named Ananias coming to place his hands on him in order to restore his sight. And in fact Ananias did come under the direction of the Holy Spirit. He wasn't too happy about it, given Saul's track record for persecuting Christians, but when he knew that was what he had been called to do, he walked right in and said, "Brother Saul, Jesus told me to do this and I'm going to do it." Boldly and compassionately he laid his hands on him, and Saul did indeed receive his sight once again.

Without even hearing Saul's account of his experiences, Ananias confirmed that it was in fact Jesus whom Saul had encountered on the way to Damascus. This same Jesus had personally appeared to Ananias to send him to Saul, and had declared that Saul would be filled with the Holy Spirit. Saul had no desire to resist. He believed this now because he had encountered Jesus. Indeed, in his heart of hearts (and this I believe is very important for us to know about Saul), for all his persecution of the church, for all his hostility toward the early Christians, in his heart of hearts I believe all Saul had ever really wanted was to know and to serve the Truth. He was simply deceived. He had simply never suspected that he would find the Truth here!

It seemed so unlikely to encounter the Truth among these social and intellectual outcasts, but here it was, or rather here *He* was, and Saul was content that his search for the Truth had been rewarded. If Jesus were in fact "the way, the truth, and the life," as He had said, then Saul was willing to give himself to this new Lord's service every bit as energetically, every bit as uncompromisingly as he had given himself to what he had previously thought to be the truth. This is what we need to recognize if we are going to understand the utter transformation that took place in the life of this man Saul.

His is a conscious and enthusiastic submission of his own will to that of Jesus Christ. That is what conversion is really all about for all of us—a conscious submission of our wills to Jesus Christ, whom we know firsthand to be the Truth. If Saul suffered for Him, if he lost his reputation or his position or his credibility for Him, what could that possibly matter? He simply wanted to serve the Truth. Here was the ultimate expression of the Truth, and it was personal (or rather *He* was personal). And this Jesus was willing to forgive Saul and take his hand and accomplish great things through him. He had chosen him, He says, to accomplish great things in His name. If Jesus Christ was truly risen from the dead, then the whole idea of a Suffering Messiah, a concept that he had previously ridiculed, made sense after all. God had, in this ingenious way, resolved the issue of mankind's sinfulness while maintaining His own holiness.

Saul the intellectual could see in this unique idea of God

suffering for our sin the answer to the most fundamental theological question: how could a sinful man stand in the presence of a holy God? In the Suffering Messiah he could see how it happened. God had taken upon himself, as Isaiah said, the sins of the world and himself suffered for our transgressions. The price for our sins was paid, and therefore He could extend His grace to us without violating His justice or compromising His holiness. It all made sense to Saul.

And I expect that the roots of that theology, which would find its expression later on in his letter to the Romans, began to take shape in his mind even there as he reflected on his traumatic experience. There was no compromising of Saul's intellect here. Quite the contrary, the Christian interpretation of things *did* make sense; it made perfect sense to him now. And Saul, once he had seen it, was utterly willing to submit to this newly discovered Truth.

In fact, he was so utterly convinced, and his intellect was still so precise and uncompromising, that he completely baffled the intelligentsia of his day by proving that Jesus had to be the Messiah. They could not refute his logic. There was simply no way to fault him or his arguments, nor to discount the facts upon which they were based. And Saul, or Paul as the Greek and Latin forms of his name read, went on to become the intellectual giant of the Christian faith.

———— ⟿ ————

Often we look at the transformation that overcame Saul's life at this moment and wonder what it takes to bring about such a radical change. How can a person be so thoroughly convinced? How could the great persecutor of the church overnight become its greatest defender? Only through a revolutionary change of heart. What is the heart of a revolution? A simple dictionary definition will tell us. A revolution is "the overthrow or renunciation of one government or ruler and the substitution of another by the governed." Paul's life underwent a revolutionary change because he substituted one ruler for another. He described the change in his life in very similar terms when he wrote to the church at Rome later on.

> Don't you know that when you offer yourselves to someone to obey him as slaves, you are slaves to the one whom you obey—whether you are slaves to sin, which leads to death, or to obedience, which leads to righteousness? But thanks be to God that, though you used to be slaves to sin, you wholeheartedly obeyed the form of teaching to which you were entrusted. You have been set free from sin and have become slaves to righteousness. (Romans 6:16-18 NIV)

He describes that transformation in his own life—"Yes, I used to serve what I thought was true; but I discovered that way only leads to destruction and death. Now I have found out what leads to life, and I have chosen wholeheartedly to serve this new Truth, this new Master in the person of Jesus Christ." That is the heart of the revolution in Saul's life.

Why do so many intelligent people reject the Christian faith? The apostle Paul seems to be an exception. I believe the reason Saul stands out is because he was willing to submit to that truth when he found it, and most people are not. He was, of course, a naturally gifted man. But it was when all his considerable talents were taken captive for the Lord Jesus Christ that he became a world-changer.

All of us, I suppose, pay lip service to our desire to know the Truth. But are we really bold enough to look for it even in unpopular places? Most are too intimidated by the prevailing consensus to honestly seek the Truth. We solemnly or noisily defend the accepted wisdom of the day as if we really believed that Truth were determined by majority vote. But truth is truth whether the majority recognizes it or not.

It is so easy to be deceived by whatever passes for truth

because it appears to serve us best in the short run. How can we be confident that we know genuine Truth? Can you be certain you would recognize Truth if it were staring you in the face?

Let me tell you what I believe is the key to recognizing the Truth. *Truth is revealed only to those who are willing to serve it when they find it!* I don't care whether you are an intellectual genius. I don't care whether you never read or care to read a philosophy book or a theology book in your life. Truth comes to those who are willing to serve it when they find it. If they are not willing to serve the truth, they are not going to find the truth.

Our encounter with Jesus Christ is unlikely to be as dramatic as Saul's. That is irrelevant. Like Saul, we will only recognize Jesus Christ as the Truth if we are willing to serve him when we find Him.

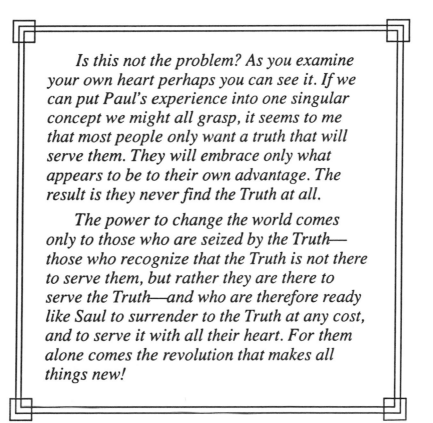

Is this not the problem? As you examine your own heart perhaps you can see it. If we can put Paul's experience into one singular concept we might all grasp, it seems to me that most people only want a truth that will serve them. They will embrace only what appears to be to their own advantage. The result is they never find the Truth at all.

The power to change the world comes only to those who are seized by the Truth—those who recognize that the Truth is not there to serve them, but rather they are there to serve the Truth—and who are therefore ready like Saul to surrender to the Truth at any cost, and to serve it with all their heart. For them alone comes the revolution that makes all things new!

A Good Man Is Hard to Find

Cornelius
(Acts 10:1–48)

Peter stood on the rooftop of the large stone house, gazing out across the aquamarine breakers of the Mediterranean at the thin blue line that separated the water from the sultry air above it. Pale blue clouds boiled up from the Great Sea, drawn irresistibly toward the white light of the desert sun now reaching its zenith directly above him. He had come up to the rooftop at midday to pray in quiet, away from the bustle of the household below him.

Peter couldn't help reflecting on the astonishing things that had been happening during the few months since his master and best friend, Jesus, had gone away.

First there had been the amazing events of Pentecost, when Jesus' closest followers had received the Holy Spirit in a spectacular fashion. Peter himself had felt a new boldness that allowed him to speak with such conviction on that occasion that literally thousands of people had come to believe in Jesus Christ.

Then he had found God's Spirit urging him to call for the healing of ill or injured persons, and found himself doing that even as his Lord Jesus had done. When called before the Sanhedrin to give account, Peter had experienced the compelling power of the Holy Spirit, enabling him to testify to the Gospel of Jesus Christ in a clear and powerful way.

Unable to slow the progress of the Christian community by *persuasion*, the authorities than attempted to silence them by *persecution*. And although Stephen had been killed, Peter himself had been miraculously delivered from prison. Most recently, as he traveled about the country meeting with and encouraging the saints, Peter had been invited to Joppa where his prayers had most astonishingly raised a woman from the dead!

Peter was overwhelmed with the evidence that God was doing something spectacular. As he looked out across the vast blue waters of the Mediterranean Sea, he could not help but wonder, "Where will it end? What will God's Spirit do next?" And the question that had come increasingly to haunt his times of quiet reflection: Was this Judaism at its best, or was this a whole new way of looking at the world?

It seemed more and more difficult to discern whether God's call was to *righteousness*, as his Jewish forebears would have affirmed, or to *faith*, which seemed the heart of this new movement of the Spirit. He couldn't imagine that God no longer demanded that His people be "good"; certainly He was concerned about their moral uprightness. Yet—on the other hand—what he was seeing seemed to go far beyond the traditional Jewish demand for law-keeping.

Peter no doubt prayed for a better understanding of God's plans, for the individuals and congregations that had begun to seek Christ, and for his own effectiveness in ministry. As the shadow on the sundial crept past noon, he became hungry and sent down a message that he would appreciate a bite to eat.

Informed that it would be awhile in preparation, Peter lay down out of the sun under the large awning, which was supported at its four corners by poles fixed into the clay roof at one corner of the house. The breeze wafting in from the water lifted the awning and dropped it again above him in a mesmerizing rhythm, as the smells of baking bread and meat drifted up from the little oven in the courtyard below.

Peter's mind wandered to his host, Simon's, occupation as a tanner and wondered how disconcerting it must be to him to be perpetually considered unclean because of his constant contact with dead animals.

As the various images melted together in the midday heat, Peter fell into a trance in which he saw "heaven opened and something like a large sheet being let down to earth by its four corners. It contained all kinds of four-footed animals, as well as reptiles of the earth and birds of the air. Then a voice told him, 'Get up, Peter. Kill and eat.'"

"Surely not, Lord!" Peter replied. "I have never eaten anything impure or unclean." The voice spoke to him a second time, "Do not call anything impure that God has made clean."

This happened three times, and immediately the sheet was taken back to heaven.

Peter drifted back to consciousness. Nothing had changed on the rooftop. The awning still flapped vacantly above him and the smell of curing animal hides drifted up to him, mingled with the aroma of cooking food. But the vividness of the images and their precise repetition convinced Peter that this was a vision coming to him from the Spirit of God. But what could it mean? "Do not call anything impure that God has made clean." Was God voiding the kosher Jewish food laws? It could be, though he failed to see the point—unless God was trying to establish a different standard by which a thing might be considered acceptable. He had certainly done stranger things!

As Peter reflected on his vision, he heard voices at the gate in the courtyard below, and suddenly he was aware that God's Spirit was telling him there were three men downstairs looking for him. They had been sent by God, and he was to accompany them on some sort of mission. When he came down and learned that they were Gentiles who had been sent to invite him to their Roman master's house, it all came together, and Peter saw in a flash that his instinctive reluctance to be found in their company must be precisely what God was addressing with his vision of a few moments before. If God was at work in the lives of these men, he must not avoid them no matter how distasteful it might be to him. He must not call anything impure that God had made clean. So he no doubt shocked his hosts by inviting these Gentiles to be his guests for lunch.

The following day, Peter headed north up the coast toward Caesarea with his new friends, taking with him six new young Christians from the congregation at Joppa. If God was doing something new, it would be good for these new Christians to witness it as well. Peter had learned the principle of mentoring or discipling from his own master, Jesus.

Joppa, which corresponds to the present day Jaffa on the outskirts of Tel Aviv, had been Israel's only attempt at a port city for most of its thousand-year history. Silt from the Nile river has straightened the Palestinian coastline to such an extent that there are no natural harbors, a fact that historically kept the people of Israel off the high seas. A rocky breakwater just offshore at Joppa provided one of the very few places where protection could be found for shipping along the coast, and thus it was here that the timbers from Lebanon were brought to shore and transported to nearby Jerusalem for building the temple during the time of Solomon and again during the rebuilding under Ezra. This was also the port from which Jonah departed in his ill-fated attempt to run away from the Lord.

But a few years before the birth of Christ, Herod the Great had built a deep artificial harbor with two massive stone break-waters at Caesarea, just thirty miles north of Joppa, and that city had subsequently displaced Joppa as a cosmopolitan center. When Judea became a Roman province in A.D. 6, the governors took up residence in this predominantly Gentile city where they could feel more at home than they did in the city of Jerusalem, steeped as it was in Hebrew tradition. Roman troops were stationed here, poised to respond to unrest anywhere in the province.

As they traveled toward the city, Peter's guests no doubt told him more about their master, Cornelius. He was a military man, a centurion in what was known as the Italian Cohort then stationed in Caesarea. A cohort was like a battalion or perhaps a regiment in the U.S. Army, consisting of roughly six hundred to a thousand men. A centurion commanded a group of one hundred soldiers, and his rank corresponded roughly to that of a company captain in our modern army. These centurions were the backbone of the Roman army, and were generally known for their courage and loyalty. They are universally spoken of in a positive way in the New Testament.

But what was particularly unique about Cornelius was that he and all his family were devout and God-fearing. All who spoke of him said the same thing. The word "devout" indicated more than inner piety. In a practical sense it suggested that he *devoted* his energy and attention toward godly activities, and we learn that indeed he did. Furthermore, among the Hebrews the phrase "God-fearing" had come to designate a person who, though not converting to the Jewish faith, was attracted by their simple monotheism in contrast to the chaos of the surrounding paganism, and was drawn as well to their ethical standards in contrast to the rampant self-indulgence of the pagans. A person who won the designation "God-fearing" usually worshiped regularly at the synagogue and had become conversant with the prayers and scripture. But in a deeper sense, a God-fearing person was one who took God seriously.

———————

Taking God seriously is more challenging today. So very few, even among the nominally religious, genuinely fear God. We live in a day when most evangelicals strive to take the fear of the Lord out of our lives and out of our worship. They say that God is our best friend, our lover, our benefactor; His Holy Spirit has given up convicting us of our sins and has become The Great Affirmer, and the Stirrer of our emotions. We will link arms and sway and sing saccharine songs that make us feel warm and fuzzy about Him, and we will scorn the legalism of those who remind us that He is the Judge of all the earth, for certainly we do not fear Him. Primitive peoples may have trembled in His presence, but we have brought Him safely under our control. He is portrayed for us, indeed, as "a tame lion."

Yet I am not so certain any lion can actually be tamed, least of all the Lion of Judah! Nor am I sure that there is any real benefit in overcoming the fear of the Lord. We do tend to become far too careless around Him. There are hundreds of quotes in the Scriptures about the importance of "the fear of God." We like to quote the proverb, "the *fear of the LORD* is the beginning of knowledge,"—a grand proverb with many profound applications, but there are many more. Listen to these: "A wise man *fears the LORD* and shuns evil, but a fool is hotheaded and reckless." "He who *fears the LORD* has a secure fortress, and for his children it will be a refuge."—a strong challenge to fathers and parents. "The *fear of the LORD* is a fountain of life, turning a man from the snares of death." "He whose walk is upright *fears the LORD*, but he whose ways are devious despises him." "The *fear of the LORD* prolongs our days." "The *fear of the LORD* leads to life and he who has it shall abide satisfied." "The angel of the LORD encamps around those *who fear him*, and he delivers them." (Isn't that a wonderful image of the value of fearing the LORD?) "What does the LORD your God require of you but to *fear the LORD* your God, to walk in all his ways, to love him, to serve the LORD your God with all your heart and with all your soul." "Who, then, is the man that *fears the LORD*? He will instruct him in the way chosen for him. He will spend his days in prosperity, and his descendants will inherit the land. The Lord confides in those *who fear him*; he makes his covenant known to them." "How great is your goodness, which you have stored up for those *who fear you*." You see, it is not a negative thing at all, is it? What wonderful promises are made to those who will take the Lord our God seriously.

This willingness to take God seriously may be thoroughly uncharacteristic of *our* day, but it is the one thing above all others that marked this man Cornelius. He was particularly notable among the Jewish population for his diligence in prayer and public worship and his generosity in support of ministry. But because he feared the Lord, he was not confident that all his best efforts would necessarily satisfy a holy God. So he continued to seek the Lord with all his heart, and to respond immediately and unequivocally to anything God might reveal to him.

Cornelius honestly wanted to know and serve the Lord, which is an attitude God always rewards. Thus it was no surprise to those closest to him when God took notice of the diligence of his prayer and worship life, and his faith, which expressed itself in such generosity. I think it would be a source of motivation for us, perhaps even inspiration, to realize that God monitors our prayer and the generosity of our giving. Our consistency in worship and our generosity in mission are clear indicators of our faith, you understand, and they do not go unnoticed by God. God was paying attention to these things in Cornelius' life as He does in ours.

In Cornelius' case, God rewarded his devotion and his generosity by providing him with an opportunity to learn what he needed to know in order to get beyond being a "good man" and to become a man acceptable to God. There is a distinction there that often escapes us. We are always wondering if we are good enough to be acceptable to God. The constant word of Scripture is "no"—we are not. We fall short; every one of us falls short of God's expectation.

How then can even the best of us come to the point where we are acceptable to God? Cornelius was a good man, but it was his genuine fear and respect for the Lord that prepared him to hear the life-changing testimony, for he knew that "good" did not necessarily mean "good enough."

When Peter and his companions arrived, Cornelius, who was overwhelmed by God's hand in all this, prostrated himself before Peter. But Peter, embarrassed, quickly urged him to stand, explaining that he was also only a man. Inside the house he explained the normal reluctance of a Jew to enter the home of a Gentile, but added that God had shown him this was wrong. "So," he concluded, "when I was sent for, I came without raising any objection. [Now] may I ask why you sent for me?"

Cornelius told once again the story of the angel who had come to him during his prayer time and informed him that God had heard his prayers and remembered his gifts to the poor, and that he was therefore to send to Joppa for a man named Peter who was staying at the house of Simon the Tanner. This Peter would give him the word of the Lord.

So Peter began to address the family and friends of Cornelius who had gathered there. "I now realize how true it is," he began, "that God does not show favoritism but accepts men from every nation who fear him and do what is right." This was a tremendous revelation then as well as now. It described the sort of people in any culture to whom God reveals himself.

We often raise that question—what does it take? Do we have to know the details of the Gospel or the right doctrine? What does it take for us to come into communion with God? Peter says that God accepts men from every nation who fear Him and do what is right. That is the preparation for God to reveal himself.

I believe it is still true today that the person who takes God seriously (God, not religion) will receive an adequate witness that will allow him to partake of God's grace.

Peter's subsequent message is abbreviated here in the text, but we can identify the crucial ingredients of the Gospel story. First of all it is the story of Jesus. Fundamentally the Gospel is the story of Jesus—not the story of religion, not the story of the church, not the story of mankind, of doctrine, of ethics—it is the story of the person of Jesus.

Secondly, the true Gospel always identifies Jesus as Lord. He is not simply a good man—not even the best man that ever lived. He is God in the flesh, and therefore Lord of all. That is the universal testimony of the Scriptures.

Third, there is a practical goal to the gospel, and it is the establishment of peace with God. No gospel is genuinely good news unless it explains how we may be reconciled with the God from whom we have become alienated through our human sin. It is the story of peace with God, and that alone brings satisfaction to our spirits. We all know people who have everything this world has to offer, but who are without that inner peace that God alone can bring as we are reconciled to Him.

Fourth, the true gospel identifies Jesus as the Messiah, the One who has been specially anointed by God. As Isaiah predicted, the Spirit of the Lord would be poured out upon the true Messiah for the purpose of preaching good news to the poor, binding up the brokenhearted, proclaiming freedom for the captives and release for prisoners, and proclaiming the year of the Lord's favor. That was the word of the prophet Isaiah, and the people saw it fulfilled in the anointing, in the outpouring of God's Spirit on the person of Jesus and on His subsequent ministry and miracles.

Jesus claimed that verse and confirmed it with His life and ministry, and that fact established His identity as the Messiah. He was not just a good man, he was in fact the only truly good man. He was utterly filled and controlled by God's Spirit.

The Gospel also includes the explanation of the crucifixion of Jesus under the curse of the law, as it suggests here—a sinless man who bore our sins in his body on the cross—and, of course, the account of the resurrection, which not only confirmed Jesus' identity beyond any doubt (here was the Author of Life himself), but became the single incident that convinced and motivated His followers to become bold witnesses to the power of their Lord.

We are compelled by the transformation in the lives of these first Christians from frightened men running from the authorities to bold witnesses challenging the powers that be. And they were inspired to this because they had eaten with, talked with, and lived with this man Jesus after he had risen from the dead. This was, certainly, the central and the only truly good news we could ever receive from God.

The Gospel includes the compelling commission to bear witness to what we know concerning the truth both of God's judgment and of His forgiveness. That would be the heart of Peter's message, and Cornelius would grasp it and understand it. The heart of the gospel is the recognition that all of us—even the very best of us—are sinners in need of forgiveness and restoration. For God demands more than goodness from us. He demands the surrender of our wills.

Of course it is only the activity of the Holy Spirit in us that can bring about such a transformation.

As Peter is speaking, these devout people are revealed by the Pentecostal outpouring of the Holy Spirit to have undergone the change of heart God's Word required for salvation. God's Spirit fills them and empowers them just as it had filled and empowered Peter to accomplish such remarkable things in the months preceding this event. Indeed, it was precisely this indwelling Spirit of God that would take each one, including Cornelius, beyond simply being "good," and allow them to participate in the astonishing renewal that God was bringing about in His world. Their baptism, identifying them as individuals who had surrendered their wills to Jesus Christ, served to confirm symbolically the change of heart that was already evident.

> *You and I, in learning what we may from Cornelius, need to recognize that our transformation begins with the willingness to take God seriously. Until we genuinely fear the Lord, there will be no change for the better in our lives.*
>
> *But what wonderful promises accompany that fear of God! If we take Him seriously, seriously enough to listen to His word of truth and respond to it, that fear of the Lord will lead us to the truth of His grace offered to us in Jesus Christ.*
>
> *Then, in the surrender of our will to Him, God's Spirit can embrace us and begin to work that transformation from the inside that alone can bring us the peace, satisfaction, and the joy that we desire.*

Let Cornelius' experience then stand as a model for us. No matter how good we may have been, no matter how bad we may have been, no matter how we might have lived our lives, may we from this moment forward begin to take God seriously and accept His grace.

An Open-Hearted Woman

Lydia
(Acts 16:6–15)

The Greek island of Samothrace, actually the tip of a great mountain submerged beneath the north end of the Aegean Sea, loomed in the bright orange sunset before the apostle Paul.

Its mile-high summit was obscured by clouds, making it appear to be precisely what the ancient Greeks called it, "Poseidon's perch," the lookout from which the god of the sea scanned the horizon for the ships that looked to him for protection.

Standing on deck, the apostle was more convinced that the God who had created earth and sea was caring for him. Seeking to establish and nurture new colonies of believers throughout Asia, Paul and his traveling companions, Silas and Timothy, had ended their cross-country trip in Troas, near the ancient city of Troy, about which Homer had written in the great Greek epics. Having been thwarted in several attempts to turn aside to the north or to the south, they had been uncertain about their next destination until God had shown Paul in a vision that they were to cross the Aegean to Macedonia.

Favorable winds had taken them to the island of Samothrace in a day. They would anchor here for the night and continue to the port of Neapolis (the modern Kavalla in northern Greece) in the morning.

It was becoming increasingly evident to Paul that God's Spirit wanted to do something in Europe. Not only had the doors to other options been closed to them consistently over the previous weeks, but after he had seen the vision inviting him to Macedonia, God had provided another traveling companion, Luke, a physician from Philippi who was intimately familiar with the area, its people and customs.

Paul was learning that God tended to reveal His will through a balance of thoughtful self-initiative and sensitivity to the Holy Spirit's leading. He still reveals himself in the same way today. We may discern his leading in our lives by considering that same balance of thoughtful self-initiative—going ahead and doing what seems right—and at the same time being sensitive to the Holy Spirit's leading, often through the opening and the closing of doors of opportunity. In any case, that is how God's Spirit consistently worked in Paul's life.

Upon their arrival at Neapolis the next day, Luke led them a dozen miles inland to the great city of Philippi, named after Philip of Macedon, the father of Alexander the Great. Two hundred years earlier the area had come under Roman rule. In 42 B.C. (as all good Shakespeare fans know) after Antony and Octavian had defeated Julius Caesar's assassins, Brutus and Cassius, here at Philippi, the city had become an official Roman colony with a large military population.

The Apostle Paul immediately recognized the strategic importance of Philippi at the eastern end of the *Via Egnatia*, the Egnatian Way, the great road that led all the way from Rome across to its terminal point in Philippi. He knew this road carried not only armies but ideas all the way to Rome and back again. It was an ideal place to launch a Christian mission in Europe, and that was precisely where God's Spirit had led him.

You and I hardly recognize this truth today, enamored with size and numbers as we are, but great movements often begin quite modestly, and that certainly proved to be the case here. The great evangelization of Europe began on a very small, quiet scale. It began with the conversion of a virtually unknown businesswoman named Lydia at a prayer meeting down along the river that flowed gently past the lovely city of Philippi in northern Greece.

One could hardly imagine a more inauspicious beginning for a movement that would ultimately reshape the Western world, a movement whose impact is evident even today, two thousand years later, because of its underlying influence on the whole structure of our government and culture!

Reading through the Book of Acts, we learn that the apostle's strategy upon entering a new city was nearly always to go to the synagogue—the place of Jewish worship—on the Sabbath. He might be asked to participate in the service, and would seek an opportunity to explain how the Old Testament prophecies had been fulfilled in Jesus Christ.

Philippi, however, was virtually without any Jewish population. Had there been a minimum of ten Jewish men in the community, they would have qualified to start a synagogue. But apparently there were not even ten Jewish men in the community. As it was, Paul learned, perhaps from Luke, who was familiar with the city, that the only worship activity in town was a prayer meeting down by the river just outside the city walls. So that is where they went on this Sabbath morning.

When the four men arrived, they found a small group of women gathered to share the appointed Jewish service of prayer. It was the most modest of Jewish worship services. You can imagine the women's excitement when they learned that their visitors included a brilliant young scholar educated by Gamaliel, who was perhaps the most highly respected rabbi of the time. As the small group sat on the grass at the riverbank listening to the moving account of the life and death and resurrection of Jesus Christ (one can only image how remarkable that sounded when the story was heard for the very first time), one woman in particular felt the movement of God's Spirit in her heart. And the movement of God's Spirit in that one woman's heart was the first stirring of a great movement that would awaken Europe and the Western world to Jesus Christ.

For a long time this woman, Lydia, a businesswoman from the very area of Asia that Paul and his companions had been prevented from entering, had faithfully sought to know the truth. When it appeared that she might find it in the highly ethical monotheism of the Jews, she had happily become a proselyte—a Gentile convert to the Jewish faith. Now (if we can borrow a phrase from Wesley) she felt her heart strangely warmed on that summer morning as Paul explained how the stunning and beautiful prophecies of Isaiah and others had been fulfilled in the compassionate and powerful person of Jesus Christ.

The whole picture began to fit together in her mind and spirit, because she had been searching for that truth for a long time. It made not only logical but spiritual and emotional sense as well. A mind genuinely open to hear the truth, even if the truth comes from unexpected places, will respond with eagerness and conviction when that truth is revealed. That was Lydia's experience on this day.

This is true of us as well. If we want to put our lives in order, we must come with the same attitude. It is an indispensable prerequisite in shaping and nurturing us for what is best: *a willingness to hear the truth*. That might seem obvious to you. You might say, "Of course! Doesn't everybody always want to know the truth?" But on the contrary, I would suggest that we seldom want to know the truth. A great number of people today consciously and willfully ignore the truth. Perhaps most of us would rather find support for the conclusions we have already drawn than really learn what is true. Finding Truth is risky business.

Current "scientific" research concerning homosexuality is a case in point. One can hardly pick up the newspaper or scan a school book on sexual behavior without reading about a genetic basis for homosexuality as if it were an established fact. But it is not an established fact. Often it appears to be little more than wishful thinking on the part of those who would defend this lifestyle.

To date, most of the major studies that purport to show a genetic basis for homosexuality have been done by persons who—by their own admission—have determined in advance what conclusions they will accept. For example, Simon LeVay, a neuroscientist with the Salk Institute of La Jolla, Calif., who supposedly found a link between homosexuality and the size of the hypothalamus in gay men, told *Newsweek* magazine that his lover's death from AIDS prompted him to find an inborn cause for homosexuality—a quest, he said, so important that he would give up his scientific career altogether if he did not find it.

LeVay admits in his study that the area of the hypothalamus affected is smaller than a snowflake and notoriously difficult to measure. No link to sexual behavior has been established and, even if it were, one could not know whether the activity came first, or the change in the brain. LeVay himself admits he has proved nothing, but the media present it as an established scientific fact, and the public is quick to accept it because so many want to believe it.

This is only one example, but it is typical of our desire to find what we want to believe rather than to find the truth at any cost. And if you and I are honest, we must admit the same is true in many areas of our own lives as well. We allow ourselves to be misled by our desire to find support for what we have already chosen to believe.

The great challenge is to be honest in our search for the truth, to be willing to hear what God has revealed in His word no matter how uncomfortable it may be and regardless of its implications.

This is where Lydia began. She was willing to give the truth an honest hearing. She truly desired to know the truth even if it challenged the relationships and customs with which she had been raised and moved her in a new direction entirely.

But there is something else of even greater importance that enabled Lydia's life to be transformed—she was willing to embrace the truth when she found it. The Bible describes this as having an "open heart" to receive the message of truth. Not only had she given the truth an *open hearing*, but she herself had an *open heart*. In that simple phrase we hear the very heart of the Christian gospel described.

The normal Greek word for "open" is *anoigo*, but the word used here in our text is the intensive form *dianoigo*, which means thoroughly and completely open—not just a little crack, not just enough to peer inside, but throwing something wide open for all to observe. It is the word Luke uses to describe the way the eyes of the two disciples were opened on the road to Emmaus, "thoroughly opened" to recognize the Lord Jesus Christ. He also uses the same word to describe the way in which Jesus had "opened" the Scriptures to them—thoroughly opened it up so they could see the whole truth and respond to it. And it is the word he chooses to describe the thorough opening of their minds to understand those scriptures.

We are told that Lydia's heart was thrown open in this same way, totally open to believe and to acknowledge the Lord Jesus Christ. It is that openness of heart that begins the transformation in our own lives.

Fundamentally, when we talk about becoming a Christian, we are talking about opening our hearts to the Lord. Having the Lord in one's heart is the definition of a true believer, and I do not believe the concept is either complicated or obscure. On the contrary, it is straightforward and unequivocal. Such a person is willing to acknowledge Jesus Christ for who He claimed to be, willing to acknowledge Him as Lord and simply and unequivocally submit his or her will to Jesus Christ. Anything less than this falls short of the Bible's definition of a Christian.

The question for us as we learn about Lydia is whether we are truly willing to open our hearts to that most important truth when we hear it, to give ourselves to it, to submit our own wills to the will of this man whom we recognize as Lord.

Lydia's baptism was her public testimony that she had embraced the truth about Jesus Christ. It was her declaration that she had "opened the door of her heart" to receive Jesus as Lord. In that very simple act, revival began in Europe, and because of Lydia's openness of heart, you and I today, drawing on our great western Christian heritage, have the opportunity to hear about Jesus Christ and respond to Him as well.

Nearly every Christian, I suppose, has seen the picture of Jesus standing in a garden knocking on a closed door. It was inspired by the verse from Revelation 3:20, "Behold! I stand at the door and knock. If anyone hears my voice and opens the door, I will come in and eat with him, and he with me." There is a knocking at the door of our hearts, and if we are willing to respond, He simply wants to come in and to commune with us, to enjoy our fellowship and let us share his company.

The picture and the verse are graphic ways of describing the action that lies at the heart of the Christian Gospel, namely the invitation for Christ to come into our lives and commune with us. It is as straightforward as opening a door and inviting someone to come inside.

Think about it. Have you ever had someone knock on the door, a long-lost friend, someone you have not seen for a long, long time? The door bell rings one day, or you hear a knocking, and there is that friend you have not seen for years, who lives clear across the country. You throw the door open and wrap your arms around him or her, overjoyed that this friend has come to share your company. That is the spirit in which Lydia came to Jesus Christ, opening the door of her life to receive Him and enjoy communion with Him. And that is the invitation extended to us as well. What wonderful blessings await us if we are willing to open our hearts to Him!

I reflect sometimes about the people that God has brought into our family's life. He has introduced us to many truly wonderful people, some of them particularly well known, some of them ordinary people who turn out to be very special. Among those who have been in our home and shared at our table are **John Perkins**, author of *Let Justice Roll Down*, founder of the Voice of Calvary ministries in Mendenhall, Mississippi, and the Harambee Center in Pasadena, California, a great man of God; **Ralph Winter**, founder of the U.S. Center for World Missions; **Don Richardson**, missionary and prolific missions author; **Elizabeth Elliot**, author, teacher, and missionary; and **Paul and Margaret Brand**, physicians and missionaries.

Perhaps the greatest blessing has come from people who may not be known in broader circles, but who are touched by God and who enrich our lives in remarkable ways through their friendship. Can you imagine how rude, to say nothing of how foolish it would be to refuse communion with these people whom God has brought into our lives? And these are all people who are our peers. Suppose it is Jesus Christ who is knocking at your door! You have the opportunity to open the door and enjoy that fellowship with Him or to say "No. I'm not interested. Go away." That is the choice with which you and I are confronted at this very moment.

The loss, of course, is even greater than we can imagine if we exclude Jesus Christ from our lives. In fact, once we have come to recognize Him at the door, the analogy takes on far more significant implications, for in this case Jesus Christ is the owner of the house and we are simply *His* guests. It would be absolute, crushing foolishness for us to bar the door to the owner and host.

Yet do you begin to see our temptation here? We may very well try to lock Him out. Finding ourselves in apparent possession of the house for a time, we may be tempted to declare our independence, to exclude the rightful owner and begin using the property for our own advantage. But sooner or later our resources begin to run out. Always of course, we would be in danger of a devastating confrontation with the true owner. And what foolishness it would be in any event, because Jesus clearly wants to share with us everything He has. He wants to teach us everything we need to know. He wants to pay for all the resources we actually need. He wants to be on hand to maintain all the good things He has given us. He wants to make our stay as enjoyable and as rewarding as it can possibly be. He has no intention of ever "sending us packing." Clearly we are far better off if He is at home with us.

But in order to maintain the myth of our independence, many of us refuse to open our hearts and our lives to Him. Lydia was an exception. Lydia, the successful businesswoman, knew that nothing in her life could enrich her more than welcoming the Lord Jesus Christ into her life; and her heart was opened that day and her life was changed.

There is another step to be considered. Having given the truth an open hearing and having an open and receptive heart are indispensable. But something else needs to be recognized as well. If we honestly open our hearts to embrace Jesus Christ as

Lord, it *must* make a difference in our lives. There *will* be tangible evidence that the Spirit of Jesus Christ is at home in us.

Lydia knew this instinctively. Her response was one of generosity. She immediately offered the hospitality of her house to Paul and his friends.

I think we see a logical sequence to the progression of Lydia's life. She gave the truth an open and honest *hearing*. Having heard the truth, she received it with an open *heart*. Her life thus changed by the presence of Christ, she responded with the generosity of an open *hearth*, a home that was thrown open to others. Having recognized that she received such generosity and grace from Jesus Christ, she knew she was wealthy enough to share his riches without reservation.

It is interesting that later on, while writing to the church in Rome about Christian character, the apostle Paul says a true Christian will be "given to hospitality." Peter also, in speaking of the sort of Christian behavior that is especially incumbent upon us all in the last days, urges us to "offer hospitality to one another without grumbling."

Presumably this is doubly important in an age of supreme self-indulgence such as our own. Hospitality is also listed among the traits that qualify a person to become a leader within the congregation. Most of us have not likely thought of hospitality as *prima facie* evidence that Jesus Christ has touched our lives, but a strong case could be made that it is in the generosity of the spirit that has received so much from Jesus Christ, a generosity naturally reflected to others, that Christ can be seen most fully.

So it is a very significant trait in the New Testament that we offer our lives, our time, our homes, our possessions, sharing these openly in the same way that Christ has shared with us.

Could it be that the prominence of this simple and tangible evidence of our faith lies in the fact that genuine generosity tests our trust in God's provision? If we can release our grip on our possessions and yet find God worthy of our trust, perhaps we can release our grip on our independence and find Him equally trustworthy. He has promised to provide and, therefore, we can be generous.

The model for our generosity, of course, is Christ himself who for our sakes became poor, so that we through his poverty might become rich, as Paul wrote to the church in Corinth. Or, later on, as he would write to the fledgling church in Philippi that grew up around Lydia and other early believers:

> If you have any encouragement from being united with Christ, if any comfort from his love, if any fellowship with the Spirit, if any tenderness and compassion, then make my joy complete by being like-minded, having the same love, being one in spirit and purpose. Do nothing out of selfish ambition or vain conceit, but in humility consider others better than yourselves. Each of you should look not only to your own interests, but also to the interests of others. Your attitude should be the same as that of Christ Jesus . . . [who he describes as our ultimate servant] Philippians 2:1–5 NIV.

The clear evidence that we have opened our hearts to Jesus is our willingness to become bold servants to one another.

CHAPTER ELEVEN

Come and Bring the Family

Philippian Jailer
(Acts 16:16–34)

There is a remarkably persistent heresy afoot today known familiarly as "the prosperity gospel." It teaches that faithfulness as a Christian guarantees us some great measure of success, particularly in the material things of life. It suggests that if we have enough faith, we can have health and wealth and good things simply by claiming them. (Some of us think that our personal experience would disprove that, although we may be accused of not having enough faith.)

I'm not sure where this "gospel" originated. It certainly did not come from Jesus, who lived with virtually nothing and died on a cross, the victim of unjust charges. Health and wealth both seem to have eluded Him. It didn't come from the Apostle James, who was beheaded for his faith, or from Jesus' brother James, the head of the church in Jerusalem, who was stoned to death. I doubt if it came from Peter, who ended his life by being crucified upside down, and I am quite certain it did not come from the apostle Paul who left us this account of his ministry in his second letter to the church at Corinth:

> Five times I received from the Jews the forty lashes minus one. Three times I was beaten with rods, once I was stoned, three times I was shipwrecked, I spent a night and a day in the open sea, I have been constantly on the move. I have been in danger from rivers, in danger from bandits, in danger from my own country-men, in danger from Gentiles—in danger in the city, in danger in the country, in danger at sea; and in danger from false brothers. I have labored and toiled and have often gone without sleep; I have known hunger and thirst and have often gone without food; I have been cold and naked. Besides everything else, I face daily the pressure of my concern for all the churches (2 Corinthians 11:24-28 NIV).

I guess the modern proponent of the prosperity Gospel would be forced to say that Jesus and the apostles just didn't have enough faith!

Truth is, a far better case could be made for an "adversity Gospel." Or perhaps we could call it a "strength-in-adversity" Gospel. Or maybe even, in our moments of greatest faith awareness, a "wonderful-things-through-adversity" Gospel, because wonderful things do come through difficult circumstances.

In any case, God has never been shy of allowing adversity in the life of a Christian. Quite the contrary (much as we hate to admit it), some of the most wonderful things—such as depth of character, sensitivity, and Christlikeness—are built into our lives as a result of adversity.

The story of the Philippian jailer is a case in point. Paul, Silas, Timothy, and Luke are still in Philippi, where Lydia had become a Christian at a little prayer gathering along the banks of the Gangites River.

Some time later, as they were on their way to the place of prayer, they were met by a slave girl who had within her a spirit or a demon that enabled her to predict the future, apparently with some success. Her owners, being no doubt good capitalists, had put this to their material advantage by having people pay to have their fortunes told.

It is fascinating and significant that evil spirits in the New Testament consistently recognized Jesus long before the people did. On this occasion this innocent and tormented girl fell in behind the foursome and began to shout, "These men are servants of the Most High God, who are telling you the way to be saved." What a remarkable thing for her to announce! You might think they would have appreciated the free advertising, and perhaps in the beginning they were surprised and pleased; but on reflection, you begin to sympathize with Paul who became particularly annoyed after several days of this.

Paul finally faced the young woman and demanded in the name of Jesus that the spirit leave her, which it did—much to the consternation of her owners who were now deprived of a significant source of income. Not surprisingly, they lodged a complaint and brought Paul and Silas before the officials who, without bothering to investigate the charges, had the two men flogged and put in prison overnight, intending to banish them from the city the next day.

The jailer, who was probably a retired Roman soldier, knew he had a couple of politically significant prisoners on his hands—different from the usual run-of-the-mill drunks, vagrants, and petty thieves. He placed them in stocks in the inner cell. The stocks were boards with leg holes that not only secured the prisoner, but could be used to stretch him into most uncomfortable and tortured positions if desired. The jailer's job, after all, was not to keep them comfortable, but to make sure they stayed where they were put.

But during the night, while Paul and Silas amazed the other prisoners and perhaps the jailer himself by praying and singing hymns there in that inner cell, there came one of the violent earthquakes to which the area is prone. In the commotion, the prison doors were flung open and the pins that chained the prisoners to the wall were shaken loose. The jailer, rushing to the darkened dungeon and finding the doors swinging freely, assumed (with some justification) that the prisoners would have seized the opportunity to escape. Given the training he had received and his discipline as a Roman soldier, the man believed he had failed to perform honorably, despite the severe extenuating circumstances, and that his only recourse was to take his own life. The apostle saw him silhouetted in the open prison doorway, drawing his sword to commit suicide. Paul shouted out, "Don't harm yourself! We are all here!"

Not only had Paul and Silas refused to take advantage of the situation themselves, but apparently they had somehow won the respect of the other prisoners, presumably through their gracious spirit in spite of their suffering, and were able to dissuade them from escaping as well! Thus they had, in effect, saved the jailer's life.

The jailer, who had resigned himself to death, was overwhelmed by this unexpected turn of events. In that moment he realized that the ideals to which he had faithfully given himself all his life, as a Roman soldier and now as a jailer, though noble, led ultimately and only to death.

These men, who were his prisoners, had something he did not have. They appeared to have a reason for living. They had hope in the midst of despair, joy in the midst of adversity—in the most appalling and unjust circumstances. Somewhere inside was a depth of joy that no torture, no mistreatment, no adversity could reach. The jailer saw all that in their lives and knew it was missing from his.

In that moment he realized he wanted what they had more than anything else in the world. Rushing in with blazing torches, he fell at their feet trembling in awe of what he saw in their lives, something he had seen nowhere else in the humanity he had encountered in his lifetime, and he asked, "Sirs, what must I do to be saved?" Perhaps he had heard that word "saved" on the lips of the servant girl. Perhaps he had heard it in the prayers or hymns that Paul and Silas were singing and praying. In any case, he wanted to know what he had to do to come to this same knowledge and to have the deep peace and joy that he saw in them.

The simple answer was, "Believe in the Lord Jesus, and you will be saved," though the phrase required significant further explanation that Paul was able to give a little later. That night everything changed for the stoic and probably somewhat cynical Roman. Through the apostle Paul, the Philippian jailer had a close encounter of the best kind with Jesus Christ, and his life would never be the same. In the beginning, he had seen Paul and Silas as chattel, or human vermin, to be beaten about and incarcerated. Now, suddenly, he realized that they were his brothers—men who felt pain and humiliation, who suffered from cold and hunger, and whose spirits could be wounded even more deeply than their bodies. He recognized the fellow humanity in them that he had not been able to see either as a Roman soldier or as a jailer.

Doing all he could to rectify what had been done wrongly, he gently washed their wounds, encouraged them, set a wonderful meal before them, and took them into his own home. And the result was that for the first time in his life he, too, came to feel the deep and genuine *joy* he had long since dismissed as a childish dream. Now here was something worth living for as well as worth dying for!

———————

For those of us who desire to share this man's experience,

it is worth noting that despite the dramatic nature of his conversion, the essential ingredients that led to the remarkable change in his life are quite precisely what they must be for us. The first was a *recognition of his need.* Up to this point, the jailer, who had apparently had a successful career, had assumed this was all there was. He had done his duty, he was successful, but when his life began to fall apart, and when he saw the strength and beauty of Paul's and Silas's lives, a particularly powerful witness in the midst of their adversity, he knew there was something missing from his own life. That is the first step in coming to Christ and receiving His grace— recognizing that there is something we need.

Second, we need to recognize that it is Jesus Christ alone who can fill the need. The jailer learned that what he desired could only be obtained by *trusting Jesus Christ for his salvation.* We must learn that we can only begin to become fully human when we surrender our wills to Him. That seems ironic to us. We don't know how we can become more fully human by surrendering our will, the very thing that seems to make us human. But it is when that will is formed in the image of Christ as it is surrendered to Him that we come to know what it is we are created for and we know that deep fulfillment not found anywhere else in our world.

Third, his conversion involved an immediate and genuine *change in his conduct.* There was an inner compulsion to do the right thing as God revealed it. This is most evident in the dramatic change in his view of Paul and Silas, the same two men he had mistreated and abused only hours earlier. Now he is willing to risk his reputation and his career if necessary to treat them with kindness and do the right thing for them. When a person is genuinely touched by God's Spirit, it will make a difference in his conduct and in his attitude toward others. Finally, this fundamental change in orientation and behavior brought him the *deep and satisfying joy* he had long since given up seeking. His life had been transformed in the most wonderful way by his encounter with Jesus Christ.

This is the heart of the Gospel, and it is always worth hearing. But we have skipped over something very central to this account. Paul didn't just tell him, "Believe in the Lord Jesus, and you will be saved," the line we often quote from verse 31. If we look at it more closely, we see that he said, "Believe in the Lord Jesus, and you will be saved—*you and your household*." Then the account goes on in verse 32 to say "they spoke the word of the Lord to him *and to all the others in his house*." Verse 33 says that "*he and all his family were baptized*." The summary statement too, in verse 34, says "he was filled with joy because he had come to believe in God—*he and his whole family*."

It seems pretty obvious that we are to recognize that the Philippian jailer's conversion had a tremendous impact on his family as well as on himself. And well it should!

In our day of cultural individualism, we often fail to recognize the significance of family and community in our lives. But the Bible suggests that what happens to us has profound implications for those closest to us as well. It is a consistent theme throughout both the Old and the New Testaments. We may not have noticed, but the text said the same thing about Lydia and her conversion back in Acts 16:15, and again about Cornelius back in Acts 10. In fact, Peter had suggested it all the way back on the Day of Pentecost, when he reminded the new believers that the promises were not only for them, but for their children as well.

What does all this mean, this emphasis on family, this suggestion that our conversion affects those closest to us? Surely one person cannot believe for another! So how is it that entire households consistently came under the influence of Jesus Christ during the early days of the church? The answer, I believe, lies in the way God has always dealt with us in community. Think back to the days of Abraham. Abraham's faith embraced his entire family, garnering God's blessing for his loved ones. The same applied to Isaac and Jacob in turn. Throughout the Old Testament we see that when a child was born into a Hebrew family, it was assumed that God's blessing rested upon that child, and that both the responsibilities and the privileges of being a part of the "chosen" community belonged to each member of the family. It was theirs by right of heredity, if you will, as they were born into a family. All the males received circumcision as an infant, receiving in their flesh the sign of the covenant God had made with their fathers before them and would make again with their children after them. Thus, the particular sign of circumcision that involved the reproductive organ.

From this, it was only one small step to Christian baptism as a sign of the covenant God was now making with the spiritual sons and daughters of Abraham. When an adult came to believe and place his or her trust entirely in Jesus, it was appropriate to receive the sign of the covenant. No less was it appropriate for a person to embrace their entire family with that sign of God's covenant blessings. Therefore, baptism was administered not only to the believer but to the family as well. For God would certainly be at work in the lives of each individual in a household surrendered to Him. This idea of a covenant into which God enters with our families has profound implications for us.

So remarkable is this promise that Paul would later write in his first letter to the church at Corinth (chapter 7), that should a husband or wife in a pagan marriage come to Christ, his or her presence would in effect "sanctify" the unbelieving mate. Moreover he would go so far as to call the children of even one believing parent, "holy." This cannot mean that all the members of the household are automatically "saved." Such a conclusion would contradict the consistent teaching of the New Testament that each person is accountable for his or her own response to God. But surely it must mean at least that God is celebrating the opening of a window into a particular family when there is at least one believer there, and through that believer, God in His covenant promise extends His blessing and His influence deep into the family, urging and inviting other members to come to Him as well. It is simply the way God works in our lives, through us and through believers in a particular family.

I am reminded of the way in which certain themes or activities tend to pervade particular families. Ken Griffey, Jr., is part of a sports family. From his earliest childhood he has had opportunity to enjoy and learn sports, and to follow the outstanding example of his father. We might look in other fields as well. The Redgrave and Fonda families produce fine actors. I doubt if it is primarily genetic. The influences and experiences and opportunities of those families draw the next generation quite naturally into acting. The Kennedys find themselves immersed in politics, for better or for worse. The Wyeths carry an incredible heritage of painting from generation to generation. Musical families are well known in history from the magnificent Johann Sebastian Bach and his progeny to contemporaries like the Simons. The Unsers produce generations of racing car drivers. Other families consistently turn out physicians, or business administrators, or military leaders, or scientists, or missionaries, or clergy. It seems obvious that there is more at play here than just physical ability. There is a pervasive sense in the home of what is important, of what is possible, of what is good. There are ample opportunities for learning and for enjoying the particular focus of an individual family. Like-minded persons who share interest and expertise in these areas are drawn together and they talk and participate together in the common interests of the family. Great role models abound. Interest in and progress by the next generation is encouraged and affirmed. It is no wonder, then, that a family grows and deepens in its shared goals, and those remarkable families illustrate this for us in powerful ways.

Every individual still chooses, of course, even though the direction of a family may be established for many generations based on the decision of one man or woman. Consider Abraham, the first person in this covenant community. His children received the sign of that covenant. Isaac, you will recall, embraced the covenant and went on to pass it along to his children. Ishmael, however, rejected it, though God did bless him just because he was Abraham's child. Isaac in turn had two sons, Jacob and Esau. Jacob chose to embrace the covenant; Esau rejected it. God blessed them both, but Jacob carried that covenant to the next generation. This is the way the covenant works: every individual must choose, but the blessing is received through the action and grace of God's Spirit within the family.

It seems a silly and tragic irony that so many parents today think they should not encourage in their children the things that they believe to be all-important. One of the great deceptions of our pluralistic and tolerant culture is that we don't believe we can hold up one particular way of life as better than any other. We believe that we cannot hold up to our children the things we think are all-important. But this, of course, is ridiculous! The New Testament knows nothing of such foolishness. Its fundamental assumption is that when you have discovered something so rich and rewarding as the walk with Jesus Christ, you'll not only come yourself, but you'll bring the family! The Philippian jailer knew that instinctively. He came to Jesus Christ through the witness of the apostle Paul, and he brought his family. Indeed, he made certain that his family was pervaded by the Spirit of God. You and I have the same challenge and the same opportunity. It should be our prayer that God's Spirit will not only touch us, but will pervade our families, in order that the next generation might know Jesus Christ and the joy that can come only through Him.

Every true Christian must have an absolute commitment to encourage and support Christian growth in the home.

If you really believe that this is the way true manhood and womanhood are expressed, if you truly believe that genuine satisfaction and accomplishment come only through Jesus Christ, if you truly believe this is the only pathway to a deep and authentic joy and peace, then it will naturally come to pervade your home and your life. It will be talked about, it will be taught to your children, it will be practiced, it will be modeled, it will be encouraged in a thousand ways every day. It will be as it is in Deuteronomy 6 where God says through Moses, I want you to talk about this with your children when you lie down and when you rise up and when you walk along the way.

It should be a pervasive thing in your home; if it is that influence will have a profound effect on the next generation. Opportunities for worship and Christian growth will be seized consistently and enthusiastically.

And if this is not the case in your home, will it be a surprise when the next generation shows no interest in continuing the faith?

CHAPTER TWELVE

How Can I Know If This Is True?

Berean Believers
(Acts 17:10–12)

I came of age during the turbulent '60s. I was a senior in high school when John F. Kennedy was assassinated and America lost its innocence. I left home in 1964 and spent four of the most formative years of my life in college while campuses across the country erupted in violence and protest. My wife and I were married at the height of the bloody and terrible Viet Nam war. My career in the church was chosen at a moment in history when the credibility of traditional institutions such as the church was at an all time low. Our first child was born a few months after the Watergate break-in had begun to escalate into a national crisis of confidence in leadership. It is, perhaps, no surprise that one of the slogans characterizing our era was the simple, two-word challenge that found its way onto bumper stickers or graffiti-covered walls across the nation: **QUESTION AUTHORITY.**

And that is what we did. Indeed, my generation has never made its peace with authority. No administration, whether

Democratic or Republican, has held our respect. We have never trusted institutions like the military or the CIA. Worse yet, we have never been comfortable exercising authority with our own children, with the result that an entire generation, it seems, has grown up essentially without discipline.

Actually, authority *does* need to be questioned. The power that comes with authority can be so easily abused. It can be used to manipulate people and undermine their God-given freedoms. Arbitrary or misinformed authority can be terribly destructive. But the implication that we should therefore *reject* all claims to authority is not only foolish, it is fatal. I don't think there is any question that for my generation, when we saw that slogan, "Question Authority," we took it to mean "Reject Authority." But, you see, that is something entirely different.

As I write this, I have on my desk a small plastic bottle with an innocuous looking clear fluid inside. The bottle and the fluid look a lot like eye drops. But on the outside label it says, with a clear assumption of authority:

WARNING—POISON—VAPOR HARMFUL
May be fatal or cause blindness if swallowed.
Cannot be made nonpoisonous.

It is perfectly legitimate for me to question the authority of those statements if I wish. Perhaps it has been mislabeled. Maybe it contains a potion that will restore my youth or increase my brain capacity. But should these particular claims prove to be true, it would clearly be fatal for me simply to reject them. So I may question authority, I may want to make sure that my authority is credible, but I will not simply reject authority.

In fact, I need that authority day by day if I am going to survive. Every day of our lives we are exposed to claims that we may choose either to observe or to reject. **WARNING: The Surgeon General has determined that smoking can be**

hazardous to your health—a fairly authoritative statement. Do you believe it? Are you going to live in a way that responds to that statement? A diet too high in cholesterol may cause serious heart problems. We have been told this on the authority of many doctors and researchers. Do we believe it? Does it make a difference in the way we live? Moderate aerobic exercise can increase your energy and extend your life. This is a good time to invest money in junk bonds. You ought to undergo triple bypass surgery. All these bits of advice have significant implications for our lives, and we will have to determine on what basis we might make some judgment concerning their credibility. Are these believable instructions or not? What will be our authority for determining how we are going to act in response to these statements?

You see, we will need some standard by which to make these judgments—some authority by which we may evaluate them. None of us can live without depending upon some authority that supersedes our own. We rely on that kind of authority when we follow a map through an unfamiliar city. We are trusting that whoever drew that map knew what he or she was drawing, and by following it we may find our way to our destination. We do it when we check the weather report before going flying or boating. We do it when we get an engineer's report about the stability of land on which we hope to build a house. We are depending upon someone's authority, and we may be investing a lot in that authority being true. We do it when we choose how we will raise and discipline our children. The outcome of that decision is terribly significant. We don't want to find out twenty years later that we have been following the wrong path entirely. We do it when we read a book on Oriental customs before traveling to Hong Kong or Thailand, to make sure we don't offend the peoples of those nations. We even do it even when we read a history book— how do we know that this is true—or when we accept the Theory of Relativity that made the nuclear age possible. In so many things we have to depend upon the authority of someone who knows more than we do concerning it.

But here is the question: If we need to depend upon some credible, external, authoritative source just for the mundane business of daily living, on what basis will we draw conclusions about ultimate things—such as the existence of God or God's nature and His purpose for our lives? What will be the standard by which we measure what is good or what is bad, by which we determine what kind of conduct is right and appropriate and what kind of conduct is wrong and destructive? On what authority will we support what we come to believe about life and death, about the possibility of life beyond the grave, about heaven and hell? What can we be confident is *true* in an ultimate sense?

The answers to all these questions, you understand, lie off the map of a material world. They are terribly significant questions, but we have no access in our world to the answers. This does not make the questions less important. On the contrary, most of us would agree they are far more important questions than those we have about the weather or about health or about our investments. But what can possibly be our source of authority on subjects like these that lie outside of the material world, but nevertheless affect how we live daily within it? Some of us like to contemplate such things, and reason them out as best we can, but is it not presumptuous of us to think we can even begin to know the truth about things like the spiritual world that we cannot see or touch or feel or smell? As the Old Testament records God's response to Job's speculation about good and evil, (something we regularly speculate about as well), he asks,

> Who is this that darkens my counsel with words without knowledge? . . . Where were you when I laid the earth's foundation . . . On what were its footings set, or who laid its cornerstone—while the morning stars

sang together? (Job 38:2,4,6–7a NIV)

God is saying, How are you going to tell me about the origin of all things, about what lies behind the material world? You weren't there. You can't observe it. You have no tools with which to measure and analyze it. How will you know what is true about these ultimate things that affect our lives in such terribly significant ways from day to day?

Thus when the apostle Paul showed up at the synagogue in Berea with an incredible story about a man who had risen from the dead, and began to talk about how this man was in fact the physical, flesh-and-blood manifestation of God, and how there was no way of ever being reconciled with God except through the acceptance of this man's personal sacrifice for sin, and that our only possibility of eternal life was through the surrender of our wills to Him, the people of Berea had to face some serious questions. They had to admit, these were very important things Paul was talking about. Was this man out of his head? Or did he know what he was talking about? Did he have access to some truth that would so profoundly affect their personal lives and their future? Could there possibly be any credibility in his fantastic words?

Of course they could have simply dismissed him at the outset. They could have assumed that there was nothing new to be learned. They could have scoffed at his outlandish claim that God had visited our world. Many people did, and didn't give Paul the time of day to explain these things. On the other hand, they could have said, "What a wonderful new teaching! What a novel concept! I like that! It's clever! I want to believe that!" without seriously examining it.

But they did neither. They did not simply reject this new teaching because it was a challenge to their thinking. Nor did they embrace it without subjecting it to rigorous testing. One could be led off down a thousand byways with that kind of gullible spirit. Instead, Luke tells us in his account, being of noble character, "more noble than the people of Thessalonica, . . . they received the message with great eagerness and examined the Scriptures every day to see if what Paul said was true." What a wonderful description of an open and yet discerning spirit! That wonderful balance is required of us all. How exciting it would be if more of us would approach life and learning with the same sort of eagerness to stretch our minds and spirits, tempered with such thoughtful reflection and good judgment. That is the phrase I hope you will take with you from this account of the Berean believers: *they received the message with great eagerness and examined the Scriptures every day to see if [it] was true.*

What is significant here, however, is that the Berean people had in their possession, (and they knew it), a trustworthy standard by which they could measure the truth of this new message, these assertions they heard from the apostle Paul. Without a standard, you realize, they would be tossed about with every new teaching. But with a dependable standard, they could test new ideas and thoughts, gleaning whatever drew them closer to the Truth. And it is clear here that the standard by which they judged what Paul had to say was the Holy Scriptures.

Now you have to ask yourself, what possible sources could there be to settle questions of ultimate purpose and destiny? What scientific or analytical resource could speak with authority about the existence of an infinite and spiritual God? Who can tell us where we came from and what happens after death? Can the scientist tell us that? Can the philosopher tell us that? Can the historian tell us that? The obvious answer would have to be, God alone could speak authoritatively about such things. And consider the implications here. If He does tell us about these things that we cannot find out on our own, then we have an impeccable source of knowledge about these most significant truths. If He does not tell us, then while we may speculate about the ultimate nature of reality and how we ought to live, the ultimate truth is past finding out. We simply won't know if God does not tell us!

Of course, the Bible claims to be just such a revelation from God. From the moment God's finger traced on stone tablets those Ten stipulations of His covenant with His people, through the conscious "thus saith the LORD" statements of the prophets, to the specific claim late in the New Testament that "all scripture is inspired by God and is profitable" for instructing us and correcting us, the Bible lays claim to firsthand knowledge of the mind of God on all the most significant things about life. The Bible says this is the source of truth for you.

Now here is the thing. We have heard the claim of scripture. You and I may either accept or reject this claim to authority. But if we reject it, we must be able to defend the alternative source of authority by which we have chosen to live. You understand that everyone lives by faith. Everyone chooses an authority to follow. Maybe we choose the Bible. Maybe we choose modern science. Maybe we choose some philosophy or some tradition, but whatever we choose, we choose on faith. We say, "This I believe is the way that will lead me to live in a proper way. This is the source of my truth."

Many people would suggest that the analytical sciences are their source of information about the truth today. Perhaps most people would suggest that. That is all well and good. I have great admiration and respect for the sciences and enjoy pursuing them myself, but I wonder if you would mind telling me what science says about what, if anything, preceded the origin of the universe? That is a very significant question. Was there something that brought this all into being? Was there a purpose behind it all? Science cannot tell you that, and any honest scientist will admit that they cannot tell you that. Science can tell you nothing about origins, for it cannot reach that far back. Astrophysicists tell us that science may trace all the way back to the "big bang," but what lies behind that, how or why matter came into being at all, the scientist cannot tell you. What does science tell you about alienation from God and the possibility of reconciliation? You may suggest that is an irrelevant question, because science proves that God does not even exist; but of course while this might be a claim of some careless scientists, science itself would never say something so preposterous. No honest scientist would say God does not exist. They may honestly say they do not know whether God exists. True science knows that it has tools to measure the physical universe alone. It has no tools for probing the possibility of a spiritual world that lies behind the physical one. Such a world may or may not exist, but science cannot address the question. If there is such a spiritual dimension to life, it is more than science can say. It is also more than science can deny. We will most certainly need some other source of authority about moral behavior, about the existence and nature of God, about life beyond the grave.

So what will that source be? The prevailing political philosophy? Do you want to base your life and your future on that? What is its authority? It is nothing more than an arbitrary and changing consensus, only briefly valid in a particular place and time. Certainly it can say nothing definitive about ultimate meaning and values. What is politically correct today is anathema tomorrow. I should not like to build my hope of life after death upon such a chimerical base.

So—again—how will you know what is true about these all-important issues if science or the reigning political philosophy cannot tell you? Will you wait for some government to tell you what to believe and how to act? Our own government keeps trying to step in and fill that void, but with increasingly frustrating results. Because it has no sufficient moral center and really does not know what it is talking about, it is regularly caught in contradictions that emerge from conflicting political agendas. So we work to preserve the life of violent criminals or the habitat of threatened birds or fish while we refuse to protect unborn and quite innocent children. Similar conflicts of official interest created the monstrosity known as the Nazi government just a generation ago. Some standard must exist by which governments too will be judged. They themselves cannot provide this authority. If not, we will continue to create the hell on earth that is so evident today in the chaos that threatens Africa and Eastern Europe.

Many people casually conclude that they will simply choose what they want to be true about life. Personal preference is their guide to the universe. A generation ago, I think no one would have considered trying to defend such a position. Wanting something to be true does not make it true, and living as though something is true when it is not can be a very dangerous enterprise indeed. The people who continue to live at the center of the nuclear disaster in Chernobyl are affected by radiation whether they want to believe it or not. And if God exists, living as though He does not is exceedingly dangerous!

You may, of course, choose some other religion or philosophy besides Christianity as your source of information about the true nature of life and the universe. Here at least we have those who claim some access to truths that lie beyond the material world, but again you must ask yourself, on what basis have I chosen this particular world and life view? You see, you must have some basis for determining what is true. Is it just because I prefer it, or because I was raised that way, or does it genuinely seem to square with reality and best explain the world I see and experience? What final authority does it claim, and is this authority credible?

All this lies behind that brief little paragraph about the people of Berea. Those people came to believe the gospel on the basis of the standard of truth that they found revealed in the Bible. Was their choice of the Bible as their standard strictly arbitrary? Or is there any evidence that would support the

Bible's claim to be the ultimate source of authority about life and truth?

The Westminster Confession of Faith reflects on the fact that experience bears out the doctrines of scripture as the best and most effective way to live. I believe that. The more we practice it, the more we find it to be true. That same confession also calls our attention to the elegance and majesty of its account of the Truth. There is a certain credibility that emerges as we read it and begin to recognize its profundity. It is different from the mythologies of Babylon and Sumer and Egypt and all the other attempts to explain the foundations of the universe.

The confession also reminds us of the consent of all its parts. This is a particularly strong and persuasive argument for the inspiration of the Scriptures, a powerful testimony to the credibility of God's Word as our authority. By contrast, say, to the Koran, which proved to be a rather self-serving document for its single author, Mohammed, though he claimed divine inspiration, the Bible is not a singular book. It is an entire library of sixty-six books, written by some forty different authors spanning sixty generations, over the course of nearly sixteen hundred years on three continents and in three different languages. It includes the works of kings and peasants, of statesmen and philosophers, of poets and politicians, of scholars and common laborers. They are writing about the most controversial issues ever addressed by the human race: questions of moral accountability and the existence of God, of the nature of humanity, the purpose of life, and what happens at death. These are topics that have inspired wildly divergent opinions from the greatest thinkers of all time. Yet the biblical writers, all these different people who were not in communication with each other, (and had no access to the Internet), speak with a common voice, giving a unified and consistent picture of life and of the universe and of what is right and what is wrong. It is a consistent story from beginning to end. That remarkable unity of the Scriptures would be inexplicable aside from the conclusion that God's Spirit inspired them all with His consistent truth!

The Bereans had lived with the Bible for a long time and had come to trust it as the sourcebook of all truth. They knew it claimed divine authorship. They saw the beauty and consistency of its picture of reality. They recognized that no other source shared its depth and unity and insight into life and reality. And they had come to learn through their own experience that in the end it provided the best way to live in the world. So they knew they could trust that book's authority, the authority by which they could evaluate any other claims to truth. What they perhaps did not recognize was the urging of the Holy Spirit to accept its claims, as they did not yet know the Holy Spirit. But I believe that Spirit was active in them as well, directing them to test Paul's conclusions on the basis of Holy Scripture.

You and I have one further and grandly compelling body of evidence in support of the Bible's claim to speak with absolute and final authority about the fundamental nature of Truth. We have the testimony of Jesus Christ, whose own credibility was established by His resurrection from the dead. In all His discussions about major issues, He treats the Bible as having final and compelling authority. "It is written . . ." He says, and the argument is considered to be resolved. There is no further court of appeal, for "the scripture cannot be broken," He informs us. He is conscious that His own teaching finds its source exclusively in the mind of God. "My doctrine is not mine," He says, "but his that sent me." "I have not spoken of myself; but the Father which sent me, he gave me a commandment, what I should say, and what I should speak . . . whatsoever I speak therefore, even as the Father said unto me, so I speak." "Heaven and earth shall pass away, but my words shall not pass away." He informed His followers that their eternal destiny depended upon whether or not, having heard His words, they now kept them. And He commissioned His disciples to explain His teachings to all those who would come after Him, promising them the Holy Spirit as their guarantee of truth. And there we have the substance of the New Testament.

Some in our day have tried to say that the Living Word, Jesus himself, is our source of truth today, superseding all of the Scriptures, but while it is partially true that He is the source of our truth, this position cannot be sustained. For one thing, we know nothing about the life and teachings of Jesus except what is revealed in the Scriptures. It is terribly important if God wants us to know the truth that He preserve that testimony in the Scriptures. That is the only way we would know about Jesus himself. Additionally, and most significantly, Jesus never stood in judgment over the Scriptures. He never said, "You know, that's actually right, what Elijah wrote here." He does not say that. There is the assumption, first of all, that all of it is true, and if you listen carefully to His words you will find that He himself consistently submitted to that word, for He knew it to be the Word of Truth. He said, "The scriptures must be fulfilled," and therefore I must conform my life to that word. The revealed Word of God, the Holy Scriptures were viewed by Jesus himself as ultimately and finally authoritative in revealing to us what is true.

This, of course, is where we must ultimately arrive also in our own consideration of the Bible as the source of truth. It is not simply a matter of curiosity that in these pages we find the ultimate truths of life and the universe revealed, that we find our questions answered here. In the end, we must recognize that it is life and joy and satisfaction for us, like Christ, to submit to these words of truth as well.

Just to know the truth is one thing. To submit our lives to that truth is something else entirely. To yield our wills moment by moment in practical ways—in the way we deal with one another, in the way we approach our marriages, our relationships, our parents or our children, our friends and our colleagues at work— this is the significant thing. To submit to the will of God, to say I will keep my temper under control through the grace of God's Spirit because it would be wrong and destructive not to do so, this is far more important than simply knowing the truth.

I cannot state strongly enough the tremendous significance of this discovery! We seem to spend our lives trying to make reality conform to our expectations or preferences when the only road to happiness and contentment is to make our expectations and preferences conform to the reality we discover in the Word of God. Jesus was the ultimate model of this willing submission to the truth.

Now the fact of the matter is that God's Word is truth, and we would not be able to resist it indefinitely in any case. We do have a choice, however. We may choose to conform to it and in so doing find joy and fulfillment for our souls; or we may choose to resist it. But since it is true, to resist it will ultimately cause us to be broken by it.

I know the choice I want to make! I trust this God who has revealed himself to us in all His holiness and all His compassion, and I choose to yield to His Word.

CHAPTER THIRTEEN

Beyond Persuasion

King Agrippa
(Acts 25:13–22)

Herod Agrippa eased himself into the ornate chair placed
for him alongside his sister Bernice at the front of the Great
Hall. He glanced around the room at the marble statues, color-
ful murals, lavish tapestries, and intricate mosaic floors that
spoke so eloquently of the wealth and influence of his great-
grandfather Herod the Great, who had built this palace.
Through the vaulted window arches, he could see the twin
towers marking the entrance to the artificial harbor Herod had
built on the Mediterranean coast—an architectural feat rivaling
the Seven Wonders of the Ancient World.

Twelve years in the building, this port city of Caesarea,
which now served as the Roman capital of the province of
Palestine, had been dedicated by his great-grandfather some
seventy years earlier to his patron, Caesar Augustus. King
Agrippa himself was not in a position, either financially or
politically, to compete with the lavish building projects and
political favors of the founder of the Herodian dynasty, which

had now served as kings for four generations. But he had learned his lesson well enough to enlarge his own capital city of Caesarea Philippi and rename it Neronius in order to honor the emperor Nero who had extended Agrippa's rule to include several significant areas of Galilee.

He knew well enough that he owed his wealth and position to the Roman overlords, even if it took considerable cleverness and the occasional sacrifice of his integrity to maintain his position as king. His father, whose name was also Herod Agrippa, had been a master of such political maneuvering. A handsome and likeable, if somewhat profligate young man, his father had seen his fortunes soar and falter, learning through the school of hard experience to cultivate the relationships that would serve him best, those that would serve to support his own agenda and aspirations. Somehow he had always been able to anticipate the political winds, and ease himself out of a losing cause while currying favor with a rising star. In this way he had stayed on the good side of four or five successive emperors in Rome. Agrippa, himself in his early thirties, had only been at this game for some ten years, but he was learning to calculate the personal implications for his own success of every decision and every relation ship in his life.

Now, as he looked around at the group gathering there in the audience chamber, he congratulated himself on his success at maneuvering into a position that could only enhance his status. Five Roman regiments were garrisoned in Caesarea, and all their commanding officers were here in full military dress, along with all the leading men of the city. This was a highly significant moment, and he was there at the center of it all. Most of them knew Agrippa only by reputation as a neighboring Jewish monarch, a figurehead necessary perhaps to the maintaining of the peace, but not really an integral part of Roman governance. From his perspective, of course, he didn't think the Romans could rule without him. They were notoriously insensitive to Jewish customs and the dynamics of Jewish life.

In fact, he didn't believe they were at all alert to the explosive situation left by the immediate past-governor Felix. These Jews were a volatile people, and Felix had repeatedly offended them by showing contempt for their customs, and more recently by attempting to stifle their intensifying rebellion with acts of torture and violence, often publicly crucifying the Zealot leaders. Agrippa knew these strong-arm tactics had not in the least lessened the rebels' resolve. In fact, it was growing. It had only driven terrorism underground. The implications were ominous. If he could not influence Roman policy toward greater moderation, he knew the lid would blow off this powder keg with such force the Romans wouldn't know what had happened.

Of course, through the force of superior arms the army could eventually put down any rebellion, but not before there was considerable bloodshed and destruction. And, as you may know from your knowledge of Masada and the Jewish rebellion, this in fact took place.

All this went through Herod Agrippa's mind as he waited for the assembly to begin. A hush began to fall over the commotion in the room, and his attention was drawn to the entrance of the new governor, Porcius Festus. Here was a no-nonsense leader with the potential to bring things back under control in Judea. Agrippa knew very little about him except that he had a reputation as a tough but fair-minded and incorruptible leader. Some Herodian sixth sense had told Agrippa this was a man with whom it would be wise to cultivate a relationship. Immediately upon his arrival in the province, good leader that he was, Festus had gone to Jerusalem to meet the religious and political leaders and get a feeling for the political climate among his new charges. As soon as the new governor returned to Caesarea, his capital, King Agrippa, who was a figurehead for the northern province of Palestine, had arranged for a visit—he wanted to be among the first to welcome him and hopefully win his support. Political connections were very important to Agrippa.

Shortly after the king arrived, the new governor had determined to get his advice on how to handle a bewildering political situation that the previous governor, Felix, had left unresolved. It involved a prisoner who had been held for two years, but whose crime Festus had been absolutely unable to discern. He was inclined to turn him loose on the spot, but the religious leaders in Jerusalem, whom he did not wish to offend, seemed to be very distraught about the whole thing. As nearly as he could determine, the issues had to do with religious matters he could not comprehend, and with some infernal dispute about a man named Jesus who the religious leaders claimed was dead, but the prisoner, a renegade rabbi named Paul, insisted was alive. Festus could make no sense of it, but Agrippa's visit had come at a propitious moment. Being Jewish after all, and something of an expert on Jewish law and customs, perhaps he could help decipher the issues and Festus could bring some kind of resolution to this issue.

During his first hearing a few days earlier, this Paul had declined to be tried by religious leaders in Jerusalem. Paul knew, though Festus didn't, that his life was in jeopardy if he returned to Jerusalem, so he had appealed to Caesar. As a result, Festus was faced with the dilemma of sending a political prisoner off to Rome (which it was Paul's right to request as a Roman citizen) without any clear idea of the charges against him. He did not want to appear frivolous to his superiors in Rome, so he had to have some way of spelling out what the issues were.

Now Agrippa had arrived and Festus had determined to hold another hearing with the prisoner to see if they could make some sense out of this and spell out some kind of charges for which Paul would stand trial in Rome. Agrippa would conduct the hearing.

That is the historical context. Now we find Agrippa before this august assembly, recognizing that this is his chance to impress the representatives of Rome and to solidify his power and influence in the province. Besides, as we detect from watching Agrippa, he really was curious about what this Paul might have to say. The cult of Jesus-worshipers was a complicating undercurrent in an already unstable political environment. His own father, Herod Agrippa I, had several run-ins with members of the cult and had been responsible for the death of Jesus' brother James. In fact, he had just launched a campaign of persecution against Jesus' followers when he was suddenly stricken down with a stomach ailment and died. Apparently the problem had not gone away in the intervening years, and now Agrippa had a chance to observe it firsthand.

Governor Festus had called the proceedings to order and explained the issues to his guests. Agrippa knew that most of the people present didn't really care much about what happened to the prisoner, and even less about the religious matters under dispute. They were there because the new governor had summoned them, and their interest was in how he would conduct his new office, and how they should relate to him. Nonetheless it provided something of a showcase for Agrippa to impress these Romans to whom he owed his political future.

The prisoner was now brought out and the room became silent. Agrippa reflected that the tough, feisty little man appeared to have been well-treated, and didn't seem in the slightest intimidated by those gathered here in the provincial capital to hear him. His dark beard and the long, curly hair that cascaded down from the fringes of his balding head contrasted with the short hair and clean-shaven faces of his Roman audience. The king could not tell for sure if he was scowling or merely squinting around the room with the weakened eyes of a compulsive scholar. Agrippa waited until the curious faces began to turn toward him and then he said to the prisoner, "You have permission to speak for yourself." Paul looked at him with a peculiar mixture of confidence and curiosity, saluted, and began his defense.

King Agrippa, I consider myself fortunate to stand
before you today as I make my defense against all the
accusations of the Jews, and especially so because you
are well acquainted with all the Jewish customs and
controversies. Therefore, I beg you to listen to me
patiently.

Agrippa was mildly surprised and not a little amused at
Paul's refusal to flatter him in the manner to which he had
grown accustomed during the ten years he had held his position as king. Usually all who spoke to him spent the first five
or ten minutes telling him how great he was. The greeting here
was courteous enough, and stated the central fact that Agrippa
alone, among all the officials who had probably heard Paul,
was likely to understand the religious issues. But he rather
appreciated the spirit of a man who would not stoop to flattery,
even when it might give him an advantage. His first impres-
sion of confidence and self-assurance in the prisoner was certainly being borne out. Paul continued:

The Jews all know the way I have lived ever since I
was a child, from the beginning of my life in my own
country, and also in Jerusalem. They have known me
for a long time and can testify, if they are willing, that
according to the strictest sect of our religion, I lived as
a Pharisee. And now it is because of my hope in what
God has promised our fathers that I am on trial today.
This is the promise our twelve tribes are hoping to see
fulfilled as they earnestly serve God day and night. O
king, it is because of this hope that the Jews are accus-
ing me. Why should any of you consider it incredible
that God raises the dead?

Well, Agrippa thought, Paul had certainly leapt to the heart
of the theological issues. Agrippa knew there had been a long-

standing dispute between the Pharisees and the Sadducees about the doctrine of the resurrection, the raising of the dead. The Pharisees, who were the most religious sect among his native people, believed in the promise of the resurrection of the dead in the last day. The Sadducees, who were more politically oriented, scoffed at the idea. The question held little interest for the king, whose concerns were strictly political, but he was curious that Paul would begin his defense here, with this disputed doctrine of the resurrection, especially knowing that Agrippa's alliance with the Sadducees, from among whom he appointed the high priest, would tend to put him on the opposite side from the apostle Paul. Why would he start with his weakest point? This was a surprise to Agrippa. Whatever else he was, this scholarly little prisoner certainly was bold. His refusal to play games or seek his own advantage was rather compelling if the truth were known. The effect was to make you take what he was saying more seriously. Clearly he, at least, believed that Truth was on his side, and that it would ultimately speak for itself. Agrippa glanced around the room to see the reaction of Paul's listeners to his challenge about the resurrection, but if they had any response they were keeping it to themselves. Their faces were impassive. Paul went on:

> I, too, was convinced that I ought to do all that was possible to oppose the name of Jesus of Nazareth. And that is just what I did in Jerusalem. On the authority of the chief priests I put many of the saints in prison, and when they were put to death, I cast my vote against them. Many a time I went from one synagogue to another to have them punished, and I tried to force them to blaspheme. In my obsession against them, I even went to foreign cities to persecute them.

That was true, although Agrippa had forgotten it—Paul's name had become so identified with the Christian cause. What would it take, Agrippa wondered, to bring about such a dramatic change in a man? From what he remembered hearing, Paul had quite a reputation in Jerusalem before this all began. He was a formidable scholar, very bright and on his way up in Jewish religious circles. His career was wide open for him. He had the best education with Gamaliel, the most respected rabbi. Why would he jeopardize his whole career by suddenly switching to the enemy's side? What could make a man risk everything to do that? Agrippa wondered. Paul was explaining:

> On one of these journeys I was going to Damascus with the authority and commission of the chief priests. About noon, O king, as I was on the road, I saw a light from heaven, brighter than the sun, blazing around me and my companions. We all fell to the ground, and I heard a voice saying to me in Aramaic, "Saul, Saul, why do you persecute me? It is hard for you to kick against the goads."
>
> Then I asked, "Who are you, Lord?"
>
> "I am Jesus, whom you are persecuting," the Lord replied. "Now get up and stand on your feet. I have appeared to you to appoint you as a servant and as a witness of what you have seen of me and what I will show you. I will rescue you from your own people and from the Gentiles. I am sending you to them to open their eyes and turn them from darkness to light, and from the power of Satan to God, so that they may receive forgiveness of sins and a place among those who are sanctified by faith in me."

Agrippa found himself intrigued by Paul's testimony. He sounded so convincing! I mean, it was such a wild story, no one would ever make it up, least of all a logical scholar of Paul's caliber. Paul had nothing to gain from such a fantastic tale, and everything to lose. Why would he tell this story, why would he risk his credibility if it wasn't really true? From what Agrippa could see, Paul had paid a great price for this and hadn't gained much at all. He had suffered the loss of all things in order to make these outlandish claims about the Christ. Rumor was that his wealthy parents had disinherited him, he had lost his credibility and influence within the Jewish community, and of course now he was on trial for his life. Now here he has a chance to escape, and he is still at it. He won't back off from that crazy story. The bottom line, of course, was the dramatic change in his own life. He had suddenly switched from being the Christian community's chief antagonist to being its chief advocate. What would motivate such a dramatic change in a man's life? Something had certainly caused Paul to change his mind so radically about this man Jesus. What could change the direction of one's life so profoundly other than the absolute conviction that he had in fact encountered the Truth? Agrippa was at a loss for an alternative answer or explanation.

Paul was addressing him again:

So then, King Agrippa, I was not disobedient to the vision from heaven. First to those in Damascus, then to those in Jerusalem and in all Judea, and to the Gentiles also, I preached that they should repent and turn to God and prove their repentance by their deeds. That is why the Jews seized me in the temple courts and tried to kill me. But I have had God's help to this very day, and so I stand here and testify to small and great alike. I am saying nothing beyond what the prophets and Moses said would happen—that the Christ would suffer and, as the first to rise from the dead, would proclaim light to his own people and to the Gentiles.

What an incredible man this was, standing there before

him. He certainly had the courage of his convictions. No one could deny that. And frankly, what he was saying rang true to what Agrippa knew! Herod Agrippa knew enough about the Scriptures to confirm that both the Law and the Prophets *had* spoken of a suffering Messiah. What if this were all true? What if this indomitable little man with the compelling logic really *had* some sort of an encounter with God? It would certainly explain the abrupt change in his personality. The very idea, the possibility of truth here began to haunt Agrippa. What did he really know about God after all? If he were honest, he certainly didn't know enough to deny the truth of what Paul was saying. And somehow he didn't doubt that the thoughtful and articulate scholar before him would be quite able to respond to any challenge he could muster.

His thoughtful reverie was interrupted by the voice of his very pragmatic host, Governor Festus. "You are out of your mind, Paul!" he shouted. "Your great learning is driving you insane." This was all so foreign to him, he couldn't make heads nor tails of what Paul was saying about prophets and messiahs and resurrections and all kinds of things he had never thought of in all his life.

But Paul was quick and controlled in his response. "I am not insane, most excellent Festus," he replied. "What I am saying is true and reasonable. The king is familiar with these things, and I can speak freely to him. I am convinced that none of this has escaped his notice, because it was not done in a corner. King Agrippa, do you believe the prophets? I know you do."

Actually, Agrippa *did* sort of believe the prophets, and he knew as well that there were no holes in Paul's argument to which he had been listening very carefully. A very credible case *could* be made linking the events in the life of Jesus with the clear and ancient predictions of the prophets. But as he looked around the room and saw all those important eyes turned expectantly toward him, waiting for his response, he was suddenly overwhelmed by the immense social and political implications of confessing sympathy with Paul's cause. He had come here after all to impress these men with his social sophistication and his political savvy. To admit that he was moved to contemplate the truth of Paul's outlandish claims would have been devastating for his image. Worse, he couldn't imagine that it would not destroy his whole career if these influential Romans saw him as gullible and credulous. I mean if anything was ever politically incorrect, it was this Jesus movement. It was simply out of the question that he could ever consider it seriously. The ramifications, you understand, for his life and reputation were simply too immense. In that moment he knew he could not confess faith in Paul's gospel. The price was too great. He had to protect his image.

With a knowing smile for the benefit of the spectators looking on, he replied probably with a condescending chuckle, "Paul, do you think that in such a short time you can persuade me to be a Christian?" But his eyes were not on Paul. His eyes were scanning the room for approval from the Very Important People gathered there.

"Short time or long—" the indomitable Paul replied, "I pray God that not only you but all who are listening to me today may become what I am, except for these chains."

Talk about chains—in his heart of hearts Agrippa knew that the chains that bound him were far more formidable than the fetters his prisoner wore on his wrists. He himself was bound by expectations. He himself was bound by a career he could not risk. He himself was bound by an image he could not jeopardize. For one brief moment he longed for the freedom and the courage of his prisoner—the freedom to consider and the courage to accept a life-transforming Truth. But it was out of the question. The implications were simply too far-reaching. Abruptly he stood to his feet, ending the interview. The good and practical governor thought the whole thing too foolish to consider, and the king's sister Bernice hadn't even thought of drawing her own conclusions. None could know the wrenching pain Agrippa felt at his rejection of what he increasingly suspected to be the truth. And none would know the profound regret he would feel in the days ahead as, trapped in his own commitment to himself, he presided over the awful demise of his own people at the hands of the Romans.

But Agrippa's experience, you understand, is not unique. The very same dynamics keep many good people from embracing the Truth of the gospel even today. You know the frustration. You know the temptation. You know the pressure of which we are speaking. Because you see it is not a question of whether or not we may be convinced of the truth of these claims, convinced by the logic of God's revelation and the events of the life of Jesus Christ. If you actually look at them, they are terribly compelling. If this were the issue, if it were simply a matter of convincing our minds, it is my conviction that every thinking person, every honest person would become a Christian. I believe the evidence is that compelling.

But you see, the question is not the satisfying of intellectual curiosity. We cannot argue some-one into the kingdom of God. The question is our willingness to humble ourselves before the revelation of God, and to take the necessary and significant risks required to follow Jesus Christ. It is a question of being bold enough to say, "Reputation be damned! I don't care what anyone thinks of me, this is the Truth and I am going to walk in the Truth, regardless of the consequences." It is a question of the courage to risk friends, relationships, popularity, lifestyle, job, reputation—all passing phenome-na—for what is true and lasting.

Agrippa did not have that courage. And the result was not only that in the end his personal dreams of grandeur and success added up to nothing—or really much worse than nothing, but in addition, through his lack of courage, he forfeited the wonder and the delight and the blessing that might have been his. Who knows the direction of history had he been willing to embrace the Truth, no matter what?

So where do we stand? Do we have the courage of our convictions? We say we have encountered the Truth and many of us have been convinced by it. Are we willing to live by that Truth regardless of the cost? It's not at all an easy road. The Apostle Paul could certainly tell you that—but I cannot imagine a more rewarding road!

Ears to Hear

~~·o~~

A Roman Soldier's Story
(Acts 28:16–31)

In his letter to the church at Philippi, the apostle Paul, was writing from prison (or more precisely, under house arrest) in Rome. In that letter he suggests that in his view, his imprisonment has served to advance the gospel. The example he gives in support of this perhaps surprising statement is that the whole palace guard has heard the Gospel and come to understand what he has to say about Jesus Christ. It would undoubtedly be instructive to look at the events that close out the book of Acts as they may have looked through the eyes of one member of that palace guard. We will do that in the form of a hypothetical letter written by such a soldier to his friend.

Flavius Ursus, to my good friend, Septius. Greetings.

A most astonishing thing has happened that I am compelled to tell you. I could not have anticipated it had I the wisdom of Minerva or the foresight of Jupiter.

You know of my recent assignment within the praetorian guard. It has been enough to make me wish to accept emeritus, collect my pension, and spend the rest of my days grooming horses or some other tolerable chore. You cannot know what it is like, Septius, to spend twelve hours a day chained by the wrist to a prisoner. Most are decidedly unpleasant. They generally smell bad and are sometimes even infested with mites or some other plague. Worst of all, however, is their generally dissolute character. I spend my days sitting with them, walking with them, listening to their profane and disagreeable conversation, even accompanying them during their necessary daily hygienic activities, such as they are.

Thus you will understand my reluctance to accept yet another such assignment, this time to guard a Jewish prisoner who had been charged with some religious crimes in Jerusalem, but who, as a Roman citizen, had appealed to Caesar. I have never served in the eastern end of the empire, but you know the reputation of the Jews here in Rome as a contentious and disagreeable people, and I must confess I expected the worst. He would almost certainly be an arrogant and abusive companion, harassing me daily with his infernal religious superiority.

You may imagine my surprise and relief, therefore, to discover that the prisoner, a man by the name of Paul, while terribly energetic, (one is tempted to say peripatetic—I am often exhausted by the end of the day simply from all the walking and pacing he does), was nonetheless thoughtful, interesting, erudite, and considerate, a most pleasant and fascinating companion.

In fact, I was thoroughly impressed by this great man and came to consider it a privilege beyond comparison to be granted unbounded access to him. You would hardly believe the various incidents he has survived, not the least of which was shipwreck in the Adriatic on his way to Rome. Yet he seems indefatigable in his commitment to spread what he calls "the gospel" of one Jesus of Nazareth whom he has come to believe is the Christ, or Messiah, predicted by the Jewish scriptures.

I must confess that I was thoroughly skeptical of his claims the first time I heard him attempt to convince the Jewish leaders from some of the synagogues here in Rome. But I will tell you, Septius, there is something powerfully compelling about a man who will suffer the loss of his freedom and repeatedly risk his life for no personal advantage but to convince you of the truth of his witness.

Essentially, his testimony is this, (and I know you will think at first that I have lost my mind, but bear with me, my friend): He claims that this man Jesus, who was crucified during an incident that arose in Jerusalem under Pontius Pilate, has come back to life again! (I told you you would think that I had lost my mind!) Actually I have spoken to my commanding officer who was stationed in Palestine at the time and he tells me there are some well-attested rumors still circulating among the members of the praetorian guard, which would tend to substantiate this. One of his friends was part of a detachment posted at Jesus' tomb to keep his fanatical followers from stealing his body, and he insists there was an earthquake that broke the seals on the tomb, and a fantastic angel appeared at the entrance, and when they looked inside the body was simply gone, leaving the grave clothes in which it was wrapped lying intact! In any case, Paul is only one of some five hundred people who claim to have seen Jesus alive.

Obviously to actually see such a thing would be most convincing, although I am afraid even then I would simply not believe my eyes. I would almost certainly think there was some other more plausible explanation. Two quite different things have convinced me. One is the compelling logic and consistency of Paul's story, and the other is the powerful testimony of his life. I have already mentioned something of his impressive life. Let me give you a brief summary of his story.

You know that the Jews believe not in a pantheon of gods such as has been our tradition, nor in the divinity of their rulers, which seems a thinly disguised grasping for power, but in a single Deity who brought the world and the heavens into exis tence and remains active in the lives of people everywhere. Between you and me, if you are going to believe in a god at all, this has always seemed more believable than all the petty, squabbling, self-serving interference of our so-called gods.

Nevertheless, the heart of Paul's claim is that God chose to visit our world—to reveal Himself clearly and to deal with the problem of evil. Presumably there might have been many ways in which He could have done this, but the most logical and effective way He could communicate with human beings was to enter our world in the form of a human being. It makes sense to me. Their prophets had predicted this—that God would visit His people in the person of the Messiah—and it is the claim of those who are now called Christians that Jesus is the fulfillment of those prophecies.

I was never familiar with their writings, but in the company of Paul I can assure you I have become something of an expert on the Jewish scriptures. Do you know, Septius, that their prophet Isaiah, writing more than seven hundred years ago, spoke of a man who, as he came directly from God, would be born of a virgin! Another prophet, Micah, announced that this man would be born in Bethle hem. Isaiah said he would launch his ministry in Galilee and that he would open the eyes of the blind, and restore the hearing of the deaf, and cause the lame to walk again. All this is true of Jesus, and is easily verifiable.

Not only that, but their scriptures also predicted remarkable details about his death. They said he would be rejected by the religious leaders in spite of the good he was doing, that he would be betrayed by a friend for the price of thirty pieces of silver, that he would be abused and humiliated, spat upon and beaten, and that his death would be by crucifixion with nails piercing his hands—and all of that took place at Jesus' death! There is even more detail than that. Paul allowed me to read about it in the Greek version of their scriptures. Their prophets even predicted he would be given vinegar to drink during his ordeal, and that onlookers would gamble for his clothing, and that bystanders would mock his hope that God would deliver him. Even my commanding officer, who witnessed his death, confirms that all this happened!

It seems to me that this is compelling evidence that Jesus really is the person their scriptures anticipated, and if this man Jesus truly was the son of God, as he claimed, then it is not really surprising at all that they could not keep him in the grave. Of course not! He would be, after all, the very source of life. They couldn't even have killed him at all if he hadn't consented to it.

And that brings up another point, Septius, perhaps

the most important point of all. You might legitimately wonder whether, if this man were actually God in human flesh, it would even be possible for him to be killed. But Paul showed me where, in the Hebrew scriptures, it was explained that this Messiah from God would suffer and die on purpose, bearing the punishment for the world's sin. So the idea was that this man Jesus would actually experience Death with a capital "D," that God would accept this as the legitimate death penalty for our sin, and then that He would actually conquer Death itself to prove that He was the Lord of Life, and could extend that life to anyone He chose, and that Death would therefore have no ultimate power over anyone identified with Jesus.

There is even more, Septius, but I cannot explain it all in this one letter. Basically what it all leads to is the possibility of a person actually participating in what they have historically called "the kingdom of God." That refers to a life lived under the sovereignty of God now, and then in perfect fulfillment and joy even beyond death.

The Jews themselves are divided over this teaching of Paul and others from Jerusalem and Antioch even though they have had enormous success establishing congregations of believers all around the Mediterranean area. Some of the Jews here have embraced the new teaching, but more have rejected it. I personally couldn't believe anyone would reject it, but these people are so self-satisfied and so reluctant to admit that there might be something they don't already know, that I know they really haven't been willing to consider it seriously.

For my part, it soon became evident that this is what I have longed for but thought was too good to be true all my life. As remarkable as it is, it really is not difficult to believe. After all, where did life in the universe come from if it did not come from God? And if God is the source of life, why could He not raise someone from the dead? And wouldn't life be ultimately stupid and useless if it only ended in death?

It also makes sense. It reveals the true God not only as all-powerful, but as holy and good as we would expect a God to be—and quite unlike all the gods we have known to date. And then it answers the parallel question of how God could take our sins seriously and still forgive us, since He suffered the death penalty on our behalf. Every other religion I know of either fails to take God's holiness seriously, or fails to take mankind's sin seriously. This new Christianity alone takes both God's holiness and our sin seriously.

I must say also, Septius, that I think the Christian way of living modeled by this man Jesus has to be the most wonderful and rewarding way to live that I can imagine. It is good without being self-righteous, noble without being insufferable, tolerant without sacrificing its standards. It finds the precise balance between giving yourself in service to others and yet recognizing your own self-worth and learning to love yourself. It finds reason for happiness and contentment even in the worst of circumstances while promising wonderful things yet to come. It offers grace without compromising goodness, compassion without sacrificing strength. Indeed to live as Jesus did draws one into a great adventure in which one finds all the breathtaking exhilaration of genuine risk while being guaranteed an ultimate security. In the end it offers the one thing for which every heart longs—a righting of all wrongs and a paradise of unimaginable pleasures— a place where things are as we have always imagined they should be.

When I compared all this to any alternative the world has to offer, there was simply no contest! One evening after Paul had been discussing these things all day, and everyone had gone home and we were alone, I asked him how I could have the contentment and joy that were so evident in his life. He said, "You know, it's really very simple. It doesn't require a mastery of difficult theological or philosophical concepts. There is no secret or sacred mystery or ritual. Believe it or not, it does not even require a record of perfect or near-perfect obedience. God knows we are not capable of living perfectly. Only He is capable of that. What it requires is an acknowledgment that we are *not* morally or physically or spiritually self-sufficient—that we regularly fail to live up to God's standards and that we need His forgiveness and assistance. Then it requires an acceptance of His offer of forgiveness through Jesus Christ, and of the necessary assistance for living as we ought through the Spirit of Jesus that He promises to place within every believer. It is as simple as that," he said.

I knew in that moment that I wanted to do that more than anything else in the world. So he prayed with me, and I just told God that I knew I was a sinner and that I wanted Him to forgive me and teach me how to trust Him.

Septius, I can't tell you how dramatically this decision has affected my life! I have a deep sense of peace and contentment that I have never experienced before. I feel clean all the way to my very soul! I have a new sense of direction in my life, and a sense of excitement, and courage, and purpose that supersedes anything I have ever known. I cannot describe to you the difference between this and the depressing and sometimes cynical charade of noble resignation to life and death that marked my life before I came to know God personally in Jesus Christ.

I don't know if anything I have said here is believable or convincing to you. I can only tell you that my own life has been delightfully and irrevocably transformed by this encounter with the Living God, and that I wish the same for you. I will gladly tell you more when you come. In fact, I suppose it would be quite impossible for you to keep me from sharing what is the most real and wonderful thing that has ever happened to me.

Greet your good wife Helena for me. I pray the blessing of the one true God upon you both.

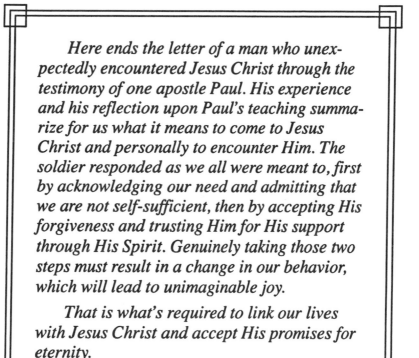

Here ends the letter of a man who unexpectedly encountered Jesus Christ through the testimony of one apostle Paul. His experience and his reflection upon Paul's teaching summarize for us what it means to come to Jesus Christ and personally to encounter Him. The soldier responded as we all were meant to, first by acknowledging our need and admitting that we are not self-sufficient, then by accepting His forgiveness and trusting Him for His support through His Spirit. Genuinely taking those two steps must result in a change in our behavior, which will lead to unimaginable joy.

That is what's required to link our lives with Jesus Christ and accept His promises for eternity.

How will you respond?

What a wonderful thing it is that we are not locked up in a universe that gives us no opportunity to encounter the Living God who made us! The central claim of the Christian faith is that in a unique and mysterious way, God has entered our world in the person of Jesus Christ for the express purpose of reestablishing the personal relationship with us that was broken by our sin. You have had the opportunity to meet him face-to-face through the experiences of those whose lives were remarkably transformed in those first, astonishing days after his historic arrival. But we might have shared the experience of thousands of others who have met him in an unbroken series of equally personal encounters stretching directly from that day to this.

One thing you may have noticed in listening to these accounts is how unique is each person's encounter with Christ. There is no standard formula, no precise ritual for coming to know him personally. Like all personal relationships, our particular encounter with Jesus will take its own shape. That is because he respects our individual differences. With Peter, Jesus went fishing. But with Nicodemus he was willing to sit down to a scholarly theological discussion. Saul's transformation was sudden and dramatic, while his colleague Nicodemus found himself moving gradually toward a recognition of what it might mean to follow Jesus.

But whatever the shape of each personal encounter, all of their experiences had certain essential things in common; they all came to recognize their own sinfulness. By contrast they recognized Jesus as the unique Son of God, the one person in a position to restore their relationship with the Father. And finally each one made a decision to change the course of his or her life by committing to follow this Jesus as Lord.

On the day of Pentecost, those who recognized their need to get back into a right relationship with God asked Peter what they should do. Peter summed it up in Acts 2:38 by saying, "Repent [which means put away your old destructive life and embark upon a new one] and be baptized, every one of you, in the name of Jesus Christ for the forgiveness of your sins. And you will receive the gift of the Holy Spirit." His promise was that the Spirit of God would actually come to live in us and empower us to live as we ought and to walk through death itself into the presence of the God who made us.

By walking that pathway through forgiveness to a new life empowered by the Holy Spirit, all these friends we have read about found wholeness and joy and purpose for their lives. And we can, too! Your encounter with the Savior is no different. It will take its own particular shape, of course, but if you are willing to return your life to His care and keeping, He will make all things new for you, just as He has for all these others.

There is no better moment to take advantage of your own close encounter with the Savior!

STUDY QUESTIONS
Chapter 1

What sort of person was Peter?

What was it about Peter that made it possible for God to change his life?

What are the three essential elements of Peter's transformation?

Why might the acknowledgment of our sins be a prerequisite to becoming reconciled with God?

How is Jesus uniquely qualified to be the only mediator between God and humankind? (How is He different from the founders of all the other great religions of the world?)

Could a Christian conversion experience be considered authentic if it did not include a change of course leading us to walk in the footsteps of Christ? What are the implications for your life?

STUDY QUESTIONS
Chapter 2

What sort of person was Matthew?

What do you think appealed to Matthew about Jesus' call? What made him receptive to the invitation?

Do you agree with the suggestion of this chapter that happiness comes from the shape of our commitments and relationships, and not from our possessions?

What does the word "repentance" mean, and how would it affect your life? (Be sure to consider both the negative and the positive side of repentance.)

Read what Jesus said in Matthew 7:13–14 and consider the implications for our society, and for your own life.

STUDY QUESTIONS
Chapter 3

What sort of person was Nicodemus?

How did Jesus honor this in his conversation with Nicodemus? Do you think God wants us to set aside our intellectual questions in order to come to Him?

Do you think the intellect is more of a help or a hindrance to faith? Why do you answer as you do? What should be the relationship of the heart and the mind?

What does the term "born again" imply?

Must a conversion experience be sudden and dramatic? Or might it sometimes be a gradual and natural development?

STUDY QUESTIONS
Chapter 4

What did Marcellus' recognition of Jesus' authority have to do with faith?

Can faith exist apart from its object? How would you define faith?

At least one theologian has defined faith as "an absolute transference of trust from ourselves to another, a complete self-surrender to God." What would convince you that Jesus was worthy of such trust? What would motivate you to transfer your trust to him? How would your life change if you were to surrender to him completely?

What is wrong with seeing faith as the confidence that we will get whatever we want?

STUDY QUESTIONS
Chapter 5

What sort of person was Thomas?

When is doubt good and when is it bad? How might skepticism help us discover the truth? How might it keep us from the truth?

How should a faith community deal with dissenting voices?

When is it appropriate simply to "stop doubting and believe"?

How can we tell if our doubts are legitimate questions, or if they are excuses for our unwillingness to make a commitment?

Is it possible to know God's blessing without submitting to him?

STUDY QUESTIONS
Chapter 6

What was it about Simon that showed his "heart was not right with God"?

What are some examples of ways in which we try to gain some personal advantage with the gospel?

Would you follow Jesus Christ if there were no immediate personal advantage in it for you? What might motivate you to follow him regardless of the cost?

What sort of heart will God honor, and what is the real heart of his promise? (Cf. Matthew 5:8) What do you think this means?

STUDY QUESTIONS
Chapter 7

What sort of person was the Ethiopian official?

How is the God of the Old Testament different from all the other "gods" we know of in history?

Describe Philip's radical perspective on the Christian Gospel. Is this Biblical? Why would it have been so difficult for the early Church to accept?

Discuss the shape and character of Philip's witness to the Ethiopian official. Why do you think it was so effective?

What was it in the spirit of the Ethiopian official that made it possible for him to hear and respond to the Gospel?

STUDY QUESTIONS
Chapter 8

What sort of person was Saul?

Why are some of Saul's colleagues referred to as pseudo-intellectuals in this chapter? Why do some intelligent people reject the Gospel?

Why does "politically correct" thinking do us such a disservice?

How was Saul's thinking changed, and why could no one ever dissuade him from his new convictions?

STUDY QUESTIONS
Chapter 9

What sort of person was Cornelius?

What does it mean to "fear the LORD," and what does God promise to those who fear Him?

What do you think is the answer to Peter's question about whether God is calling us to righteousness, or to faith? What was the evidence of Cornelius' faith?

The word "gospel" means "good news." What is the good news at the heart of the Gospel story?

Contrary to popular opinion, Christianity is not about "being good." What is it about?

STUDY QUESTIONS
Chapter 10

How did God reveal His will to Paul? Do you think this is how He still reveals His will today? Have you had any experience with this?

Where did the awakening of Europe and the Western world to Jesus Christ begin?

Tell about Lydia's search and describe the awakening of God's Spirit in her heart.

Do you think you are genuinely open to hearing and responding to the truth, no matter what it is? What might cause you to fear the truth? What might motivate you to overcome your fear?

How should our acceptance of Christ's unconditional love for us affect the way we treat other people?

STUDY QUESTIONS
Chapter 11

Why can the "prosperity gospel" not be supported from scripture?

What do you think was so appealing to the jailer about the faith of Paul and Silas?

Discuss the essential steps in the Philippian jailer's transformation. Can a person become a Christian without walking through each of these steps?

What should be the impact of your personal faith on your family and those closest to you? How is that most likely to come about?

STUDY QUESTIONS
Chapter 12

What is the difference between questioning and rejecting authority? Why is some credible authority absolutely necessary for our lives?

What possible authority could we ever find for truths that lie beyond the reach of the observable world? (Questions about the nature of God, or origins, or death, or morality, for instance.) What are the implications for our lives if these truths are inaccessible to us?

How may we evaluate the various sources that suggest themselves to us as authorities on these deeper questions of purpose and destiny? How does the Bible "stack up" when we submit it to these evaluative criteria?

What risks do you face if you submit to the authority of the Bible? What risks do you face if you submit to some other authority?

STUDY QUESTIONS
Chapter 13

What do you find convincing about Paul's testimony?

What might it have cost Agrippa to accept the Christian faith?

What did it cost him to reject it?

What are the chains that seem to restrict your freedom to accept the Christian Gospel? What do you stand to gain or lose by accepting or rejecting it?

STUDY QUESTIONS
Chapter 14

What are some of the things which convinced the Roman soldier to commit his life to Jesus Christ?

Compare the world's alternatives to those things the soldier found so compelling. In the end, what did his commitment involve? What was the effect upon his life? What would it take to convince you to commit your life to Jesus Christ?

Aharoni, Yohanan and Michael Avi-Yonah. Prepared by Carts, Ltd. *The MacMillan Bible Atlas*. (New York: MacMillan Publishing Co., Inc.,) 1968.

Alexander, David and Pat, ed. *Eerdmans' Handbook to the Bible*. Grand Rapids, Michigan: William B. Eerdmans Publishing, 1973.

Barclay, William. *The Acts of the Apostles*. Philadelphia: The Westminster Press, 1956.

————. *The Gospel of John*. Vol. 1 & 2, Philadelphia: The Westminster Press, 1958, *The Gospel of Luke*. Philadelphia: The Westminster Press, 1956.

————. *The Gospel of Mark*. Philadelphia: The Westminster Press, 1956.

————. *The Gospel of Matthew*. Vol. 1, Philadelphia: The Westminster Press, 1958.

Berkhof, L, *Systematic Theology*. Grand Rapids, Michigan: William. B. Eerdmans Publishing, 1941.

Blaiklock, E.M. *Tyndale New Testament Commentaries: The Acts of the Apostles*. Grand Rapids, Michigan: William B. Eerdmans Publishing Company, 1959.

Book of Confessions of the Presbyterian Church (U.S.A.), Part I. 1994.

Bowra, C.M. *Great Ages of Man: Classical Greece*. Alexandria, Virginia: Time-Life Books, 1965.

Bridge, Donald and David Phypers. *The Water that Divides: The Baptism Debate*. Downers Grove, Illinois: InterVarsity Press, 1977.

Bromiley, Geoffrey W. *Children of Promise: The Case for Baptizing Infants*. Grand Rapids, Michigan: William B. Eerdmans Publishing, 1979.

Bruce, F.F. *Jesus and Paul: Places They Knew*. Nashville, Tennessee: Thomas Nelson, Inc., 1981.

————. *The New International Commentary on the New Testament: The Book of the Acts*. Grand Rapids, Michigan: William. B. Eerdmans Publishing, 1954.

————. *New Testament History*. Garden City, N.Y.: Doubleday & Company, Inc., 1969.

————. *Paul: Apostle of the Heart Set Free*. Grand Rapids, Michigan: William B. Eerdmans Publishing, 1977.

Casson, Lionel. *Great Ages Of Man: Ancient Egypt*. Alexandria, Virginia: Time-Life Books, 1965.

Dallas, Joe. "Born Gay". *Christianity Today*. Vol. 36, No. 7, 22 June 1992, 20–23.

Durant, Will. *The Story of Civilization: Part I Our Oriental Heritage*. New York: Simon and Schuster, 1963.

Edersheim, Alfred. *The Life and Times of Jesus the Messiah*. Vol. 1 & 2. McLean, Virginia: MacDonald Publishing Company, n.d.

Gower, Ralph. *The New Manners and Customs of Bible Times*. Chicago: Moody Press, 1987.

————. *New Testament Commentary: Exposition of the Gospel According to Matthew*. Grand Rapids, Michigan: Baker Book House, 1973.

Hendriksen, William. *New Testament Commentary: Exposition of the Gospel According to Luke*. Grand Rapids, Michigan: Baker Book House, 1978.

 Rapids, Michigan' Baker Book House, 1973.

Jastrow, Robert. *God and the Astronomers*. New York: W.W. Norton & Company, Inc., 1978.

Jeremias, Joachim. *Jerusalem in the Time of Jesus*. Translated by F.H. and C.H. Cave. Philadelphia: Fortress Press, 1969.

Lane, William L. *The Gospel According to Mark,* Grand Rapids, Michigan: William. B. Eerdmans Publishing, 1974.

McDowell, Josh. *Evidence That Demands a Verdict: Historical Evidences for the Christian Faith*. San Bernardino, California. Campus Crusade for Christ, Inc., 1972.

Morris, Leon. *The Gospel According to John*. Grand Rapids, Michigan: William. B. Eerdmans Publishing, 1973.

National Geographic Society. *Everyday Life in Bible Times*. A volume in the Story of Man Library prepared by National Geographic Book Service, 1967.

———. *Greece and Rome Builders of Our World*. A volume in the Story of Man Library prepared by National Geographic Book Service, 1968.

Palmer, Earl F. *The Intimate Gospel: Studies in John*. Waco, Texas: Word Books, 1978.

Rogerson, John. *Atlas of the Bible*. New York: Facts on File, 1985.

Smith, Paul. *Jesus: Meet Him Again For the First Time*. Gresham, Oregon: Vision House Publishing, Inc., 1994.

Stott, John R.W. *Basic Christianity,* Grand Rapids, Michigan: William. B. Eerdmans Publishing, 1958.

Tenney, Merrill C. *New Testament Survey*. Grand Rapids, Michigan: William. B. Eerdmans Publishing, Inc., 1961.

Thompson, J.A. *Handbook of Life in Bible Times*. Downers Grove, Illinois: Inter-Varsity Press, 1986.

Webster, Douglas D. *Selling Jesus: What's Wrong with Marketing the Church*. Downers Grove, Illinois: InterVarsity Press, 1992.